GARDEN DESIGN
PRACTICAL ADVICE FOR PROFESSIONAL RESULTS

ALI WARD

BBC

Published by
BBC Worldwide Limited,
Woodlands, 80 Wood Lane,
London W12 0TT

First published 2001
Text and illustrations
copyright © Ali Ward 2001

For credits for all other
photographs, see p160.

ISBN: 0 563 53707 8

Commissioning Editor
Vivien Bowler
Project Editor
Helena Caldon
Art Direction
Cover: Pene Parker
Book: Lisa Pettibone
Design
Andrew Barron and Collis
Clements Associates
Illustrations
Ali Ward
Picture Research
Rachel Jordan

Typeset in Italian Garamond
and Quay Sans

Printed and bound in
Italy by Chromo Litho Ltd

Colour separations by
Kestrel Digital Colour,
Chelmsford

This book is dedicated to Grandad Walter
who first handed me a trowel

Acknowledgements
With special thanks to
Viv Bowler for her
enthusiasm and constant
guiding hand.
Helena Caldon, Andrew
Barron and Rachel Jordan —
the team of professionals
who between them turned
the book in my mind's eye
into reality.
Amanda Eichler, who hates
gardening but typed every
word, thank you for your
irreverent comments that
kept me from taking myself
too seriously.
Lastly to my partner, Mark,
and baby daughter, Sorrel,
who was born whilst I was
writing this book.

CONTENTS

Introduction *6*

Inspiration *10*

The Bones of the Garden *20*

Features and Structures *32*

Boundaries *46*

Water *58*

Designing with Plants *72*

Getting Started: the Practicalities *100*

THE GARDEN DESIGNS

A Stylish Minimal Garden *116*

A Suburban Family Garden *120*

A City Roof Garden *124*

An Organic Vegetable Garden *128*

A Garden for the Senses *132*

A Wildlife Garden *136*

A Coastal Garden *140*

A Garden for the Disabled *144*

Adapting the Designs *148*

Practical Points *154*

Suppliers' Directory *156*

Index *158*

INTRODUCTION

I can trace my horticultural heritage back through several generations of passionate amateur gardeners. If I were a pedigree cat, I would definitely be Grand Champion material.

The smell of a Swan Vesta burnt until it was all but charcoal, the rattle of seeds in an empty Three Nuns tin still with a whiff of tobacco scent, and the heady mix of a cedar-wood greenhouse with pungent pelargoniums are enough to whisk me back to my earliest memories of pricking out seedlings on the floor of Grandad's greenhouse. Even as a child I loved the patience required to be a good gardener, waiting for a seed to germinate, pricking it out and growing it on, then finally planting out regimented rows of red sage and blue lobelia, a style that was so much the fashion in the sixties.

Sadly Grandad died before he saw me take up horticulture as a career. He was proud of everything I did, but his joy would have been unbounded if he knew I had followed in Percy's footsteps. Maybe he is up above now, hoeing a cloud with Mr Thrower.

My search for a career in horticulture began when my wanderlust waned. I realized that my vocation as a fashion model would not last much past the age of twenty-five. With so much to learn, the only way to get to grips with the subject and gain the respect of my peers would be to start at the bottom and so, armed with a copy of the RHS *Encyclopaedia of Plants and Flowers* and an advert in the local paper, I collected enough clients to keep me mowing and weeding all year round. I set myself the task of learning one new plant every day and, 1,095 plants later and with enormous biceps, skin the colour of a saddle bag and not a fingernail to call my own, I began a course in garden design. While learning to create planting schemes and draw plans was enjoyable, I revelled in the practical soil science, identification of pests and diseases and even in surveying, apart from the fact that it always rained during surveying practice.

Now I feel like one of the luckiest people alive: my job is also my passion – or is it vice versa? In my private practice I design very much with people in mind. Developing a square of land into a beautiful garden is quite easy, but creating a garden that captures the hopes, loves and needs of a client is the greatest challenge.

With this book I want to teach you how to use the skills of a garden designer to create your own garden. Perhaps I can remove some of the mystique and simplify the process. I would like to imagine this book in a few years' time, slightly dog-eared and with lots of the corners turned over where you have returned to consult it again and again. The thought that it might remain pristine and crisp on a shelf is not appealing, for I am a hands-on designer and I want you to be the same. Read this book, then get outside and get on with it.

The latter part of this book deals with eight hypothetical clients, covering a variety of ages, styles and financial constraints. Although they exist only within my imagination, I have got to know all of the households and applied the principles of 'Have', 'Want' and 'Need' to each garden design. What do the clients already have in their gardens, and is anything worth keeping? What do they really want, letting imagination run riot and throwing budgets to the wind? And, finally, what do they actually need, the nitty-gritty boring part: considerations of washing lines, pets and unsightly views.

Each of these designs is drawn in plan form and then translated into an isometric drawing, giving a three-dimensional view of the finished garden. There are complete planting plans for each garden and suggestions on how to take inspiration from the designs and apply some of the elements to your own garden. At the end of the book I have also adapted each of these plans to fit a garden of an awkward shape.

Within the rest of the book I have tried to take my life-long love of horticulture and combine it with the knowledge I have collected as a gardener and designer, breaking down all of the elements of good design practice, from selecting suitable hard landscape materials through inspirational sources to surveying and laying out. I'm not suggesting that one read of this book will turn you into a great garden designer, but I hope that it will help you to teach yourself the skills needed to design your own garden. Use it as a source of inspiration and encouragement to create something that is 100 per cent your own design. When you get lost along the way, I hope you will pick my book up and get some guidance to clear your mind.

Whatever you do, never lose sight of the joy of gardening. Don't get so wrapped up in attaining perfection that you forget to appreciate the smell of grass after it has just been cut or the crumpled paper petals of a newly opened poppy.

Remember to enjoy the journey of creating a garden. It might be a very long one; in fact your destination may always be just around the next corner.

Ali Ward

INSPIRATION

Chances are that when it comes to the style of garden you are aiming for, you will fall into one of two categories. You will either have a very firm picture in your mind of exactly how you would like your design to look or, more likely, you will have some idea of what you *don't* want and several thoughts on things you would like to incorporate. If you are like me, what you want might veer from minimalist elegance to cluttered cottage-style depending on what sort of mood you are in, but unless you really desire a neo-classical, postmodern, Tudoresque, medieval-revival, art-deco mix, you need to refine your ideas.

There is little mystery in good design: it is something that all of us do each day, almost without knowing it. Arranging the furniture in a room or making up your face both require a subliminal artistic eye. As children we are encouraged to express ourselves in art, from painting with our fingers and modelling clay to cutting out and sticking paper shapes, but as we get older the fear of not being good enough takes away the desire to express ourselves artistically. Design is not rocket science. Using a few simple rules and taking inspiration from many sources, anyone can have a good stab at it. So in order to become a designer you need to put away your inhibitions, get out the crayons and try to find the child inside you that loved to draw. Personally I would like to advocate colouring-in as a daily stress-buster as well as an outlet for artistic talent.

Get close to your plants. The spiral centre of this *Echeverium* (above) creates an inspiring shape.

(Opposite) I find sculptural qualities in many plants. The twisting bark on this sweet chestnut is worthy of inspection.

Before you can design your garden, and before we get bogged down with rules and practicalities, you need to collect together objects, cuttings, pictures and words that appeal to you. Not necessarily linked to gardening, they may contain colours or textures or tactile qualities that you like; but don't be too literal. Arrange these items on your desk or stick them to a piece of board. This is your inspirational reminder. Keep it to hand while you are designing, to refer back to. As you choose things for your board you will find that you have already begun to refine your ideas. There will be colours or materials that crop up again and again.

While I would never advocate plagiarizing other designers' work, you can certainly glean inspiration for your garden from their talented approach. To say that there is no such thing as a new idea is a tired phrase; it was better expressed by the fashion design icon Coco Chanel, who said, 'Those who believe in their own originality have a very short memory.' As each generation of designers reaps ideas from the past and then shapes and adapts them in their own form, they add a little style from their own era.

One of the reasons why design of every sort has recurring themes down the generations is that there are some basic rules. Don't turn the page just because it sounds like I'm getting to the boring bit – the Rule of Ratio is worth understanding because it will really help you later.

This magic ratio, displayed in various objects from the Parthenon to the petals of a flower, was defined by a thirteenth-century mathematician called Leonardo Fibonacci. He solved a problem that had fascinated scholars for years. This was to find out, starting with one pair of rabbits, how many pairs would be born in an enclosed place in the course of a year. The following

Salix – one of my favourite garden materials. It is used here in an amazingly imaginative way to create bridges, towers and spheres. Take an ordinary material like willow, and interpret it in a new style.

sequence of numbers resulted: 1, 2, 3, 5, 8, 13, 21, 34, 55, 89, 144, 233, and so on. When he analyzed the figures, Fibonacci realized that each number was the sum of the two preceding numbers. Students of the sequence discovered that each number bears a special relationship to the numbers surrounding it. Divide a Fibonacci number, after the fourteenth number in the sequence, by the next highest number and the result is 0.618034. This proportion, 0.618034 to 1, is the mathematical basis for the Parthenon, the arrangement of petals on a sunflower and the great spiral galaxies of outer space. The Greeks based much of their art and architecture upon it, calling it 'the golden mean'. The golden mean is a proportion of 1:0.618 or, more roughly, the 'one-third: two-thirds rule'. When you are dividing a garden into individual compartments for terrace, beds or lawn, the use of the golden mean will always generate patterns of pleasing proportion.

In a natural landscape setting, poetry provides the human presence.

There is one factor that will make your garden design unique, and that is you. A garden must reflect the personality of its owner. Strive to make your mark on the landscape. You will do this by your choices of materials and colours, but try to think more literally about making the garden an individual space. If you are passionate about poetry, have a significant line of verse carved in a pergola beam or put the date when you created the garden in pebble mosaic in a step. I once designed a box garden in the shape of a DNA double helix for a customer who was a scientist and an outside four-poster bed for a couple who loved to love. Make your garden as unique as you. Gardens are emotional places. Mine is a source of comfort when

VERVM HAEC TANTVM ALLA⸱⸱⸱TER CAPVT EXTVLIT VRB⸱ O⸱⸱TVM LENTA SOLE⸱⸱⸱NTER VIBVRNA CVPRESSI

I am upset and somewhere that lifts my spirits on a daily basis. During the first meeting I have with a new client I always ask them to close their eyes and imagine themselves in their finished garden. Then I ask them to give me three words that explain how they feel there. The answers are very useful when I am forming their design and more telling than any straight and practical

The 1997 Chelsea gold medal-winning garden, by Christopher Bradley-Hole, shows the use of Virgil's poetry in an ochre-coloured wall recessed behind vivid purple planting.

responses. The answers I have had include calm, moist, euphoric, relaxed and asleep. Try this for your own garden to establish the atmosphere you wish to achieve.

Somewhere between imagination and practical requirements are the 'Have', 'Want' and 'Need' lists. These are essential for finding out what your garden has to do for you. Try to include every member of the household when compiling the lists. Everyone will have different needs to be catered for. First, write a list of what you have in the garden. Include information on the size, shape and aspect of your plot. Add any features that are already in your garden, such as trees you would like to keep, or a terrace. Then write down your wants. Try not to be too practical at this stage. Let your imagination run riot: include features you would like, such as a pergola or summer house, water feature or terrace, as well as items such as children's play equipment and a lawn. Then write down what you *need* for the garden. Hopefully this will overlap with your wants, but will also include the more mundane requirements such as a washing line, bin space and dog kennel.

If you are short of ideas for your 'Want' list, why not visit well-known, established gardens for inspiration? Historical garden reference can be very influential for today's designers especially if, like me, you are an old romantic who longs for a classical garden of topiary, parterres and follies. These gardens often covered acres, took years (not to mention family fortunes) to construct and, in some cases, like Chatsworth in Derbyshire, involved the moving of a whole village because it spoiled the view. Drawing inspiration from Chatsworth might seem a bit over-ambitious, but we can still glean ideas for our own modest plots. Imagine Chatsworth's great cascade scaled down to a small stepped rill in a sloping garden, or the temple

lawn at Anglesey Abbey in Cambridgeshire reduced in size to
create a small secluded seating area within a domestic garden
design – though we would perhaps not have room for replicas
of the Abbey's life-size statues of resting lions.

Putting gardens aside, I often find inspiration in the work
of talented artists from other fields. William Morris, the great

Enormous landscapes that
seem to go on forever can
still inspire small gardens.
A stream of fresh water
across this Norfolk beach
gives me ideas for shape
and proportion.

Arts and Crafts designer, produced intricate wallpaper and fabric designs in subtle shades. These can be simplified and translated into mosaic patterns for terraces or used purely as a guide for colour combinations in border planting schemes.

I have always admired the way in which the Scottish designer Charles Rennie Mackintosh used lines in a bold and inspiring fashion. Imagine his classic rose motif as a garden design. The rose becomes the shape of the terrace in several tones of cobbles, the stem becomes a path and the background becomes flower borders, with the addition of a pergola surrounding the garden as a frame. Mackintosh just designed your garden for you.

Further afield, the great American architect Frank Lloyd Wright had an inspiring outlook on design. When looking at his work, you can see how he used materials that were sympathetic to their situation. His designs blend so well with their surroundings it is often hard to see where the building ends and the garden begins. His designs appear to grow from their foundations as if they developed there by themselves. This joining of house and garden has been practised in many forms, from Islamic gardens enclosed on all sides for protection and looking to all intents and purposes like another room in the house, through to parterres that were made to be viewed from the great houses, blending the parks surrounding the estate into the house.

Visit as many different styles of houses and gardens as you can, looking with new eyes at the way designers have developed a site. Even if you don't like what they have done, you can always learn from their techniques. Sometimes knowing what you don't want is half the battle.

The master of subtle colour combinations, William Morris shows great varieties of green and blue in this section of one of his famous wallpaper designs.

Fibonacci's golden mean can be seen to perfection in the tightly packed flower buds on this *Allium sphaerocephalon* head. Don't forget to get right up to your plants, they are even more beautiful when viewed from a few millimetres.

THE BONES
OF THE GARDEN

The bones of the garden are just that: the hard landscaping materials of paths, terraces and decks form the skeleton of the garden on which your entire design will hang. You will know if you have the makings of a great design if your garden looks good with just these bones. However, in order to achieve this they must be perfectly proportioned and well constructed.

DECKS

Borrowed from the Americans, the deck is an extension on the idea of a veranda, a wooden shelf that protrudes from the main inside living area, with relaxing seats, railings and a sloped wooden canopy overhead. More often than not, American verandas are on the front of a property, allowing you to sit and watch the world passing your door, but I favour its use in the back garden, where there is more privacy.

It has to be said that the deck has recently been done to death and some of the ready-made kit forms are extremely unattractive. With these 'off-the-peg' decks the two most common problems are their siting and their colour. We are in the realms of orange wood stain. Admittedly the colour will fade in time, but life is short, so I would stain the wood a more pleasing shade or, whenever possible, purchase the deck unstained so that you can start from scratch. As for siting, when a deck comes as a ready-made unit the dimensions of your feature are already decided so you have to make sure that it is in harmony with its surroundings. Don't just plonk it on a lawn.

The boards of this deck (above) run away from the eye, giving an elongated vista.

(Opposite) Enclosure is an immensely important part of gardening design. It creates secluded areas and gives you the chance to grow a wonderful range of climbers.

Line it up with paths or vistas, nestle it among existing trees or borders and ensure that it is large enough to accommodate your table and chairs.

A bespoke deck, on the other hand, is a thing of beauty and infinite possibilities. You are not limited by the size of your building unit as you are when using, say, stone or brick. Planks can be any width and can be used to create wonderful sweeping curves and circles. Try to get away from square decks. Even within a deck shape the wooden planks can create herringbone or sunray effects, increasing the opportunities for attractive design.

Decks really come into their own in a garden with changes of level. Most decks are constructed on timber legs, and by lengthening or shortening these you can accommodate any size of slope without the need for the major earth works and foundations that a stone terrace would require. On an extremely steep slope a deck can provide beautiful steps and terraces, turning a problem site into a magnificent wooden amphitheatre. (See 'A Coastal Garden' on page 140 for a deck on more than one level.)

When designing your deck shape there are various features that can be incorporated into the basic structure. Integral seating, such as the low wooden couch in 'A City Roof Garden' on page 124, will mean there is always somewhere to sit without the tiresome need to get out chairs. A pergola can easily be included if the foundation legs of a deck are left to protrude above the deck level, providing supports for a timber roof or simple rope swags.

PATHS

Paths can be the disaster area of a garden design. Everyone has them, most of them are necessary, but very few are aesthetically pleasing or technically correct. They are an artistic tool by which the garden designer can control the movements of the viewer,

By turning inexpensive garden slabs at an angle and by using two sizes of slab, a humble material can create an exciting and practical path.

Combining a deck and a pergola, both in natural wood and draped with roses, has created the most subtle and romantic resting place. The stream is a bonus, but it would work equally well with a less extravagant water feature.

leading them on a route around the garden. They can regulate the speed and style of your perambulation, the ease of passage and the view available. A path that is narrow and winding, where the plants lean from their borders on to the passageway, will encourage you to travel slowly, to stop and look at the plants and enjoy your journey. A smooth, wide path with a 'reward' at its end, on the other hand, tempts you to stride forth and explore.

First, however, technical design expertise is essential with paths. I could scream every time I see a pathway that goes nowhere. Why bother? A path must have a reason. Where is it taking you? Can you continue along the path so that a route is created around the garden? Even if your garden is minute, you ought to be able to saunter round.

Next comes the practical planning of your path's materials. If there is already an area of terrace or deck from which your path emanates, you may choose to echo the material in your path, giving continuity to the design. Alternatively you may mix in a second material to allow you artistic flair. For example, a brick terrace can be extended with a brick and slate path or perhaps brick and grass. You can choose to have an entirely new hard material for your path, but be careful – a paving-catalogue effect can result if you mix too many materials together. Try to retain continuity in the colour or texture.

Path surfaces dictate the type of access that they facilitate. Deep gravel will be no good for a child riding a bicycle, and will make pushing a wheelchair next to impossible. Small individual paving units require high maintenance, each crack harbouring weeds, while large slabs are not only easier to lay, but also to maintain. It is worth designing your path width to fit your chosen paving unit. For example, if you are using slabs of 60x60cm (2x2ft) you can make your path 60cm (2ft), 120cm (4ft) or

180cm (6ft) wide so that there is no need to cut the slabs, as the path will be exactly divisible by the dimensions of the slabs.

Even if you are pushed for space, don't skimp too much on path width. The minimum for a comfortable walk is 60cm (2ft), but the path should be wider if you don't want to become intimate with anyone coming the other way.

A path need not be a solid run of hard landscape. Stepping stones can lead the eye and provide a route across a lawn without getting your feet wet. Always lay your stones and walk on them before bedding them in. They should be placed to allow an easy stroll. Make this right for you – my own stones are often too wide apart for clients as I have rather long legs. Also make sure each step is big enough for your feet: one brick will be too small.

A path can be as informal as a stretch of mown grass through riotous planting. The end of this route is hidden to give the impression of greater space.

LAWNS

There seems to be an increasing trend to do away with lawns, mostly under the pretext of making a garden easier to maintain. While I agree that the twice-weekly mid-summer grass mowing can be a bind, the rewards of this much-neglected and hard-working plant can so easily be overlooked. For any garden of a good size the usefulness of a lawn for a family with children is indisputable, even if it is used only as a games pitch until all traces of green have been replaced by mud.

As a design feature a lawn can be invaluable. How many other of your garden plants provide lush green swathes in mid-winter? With a little care and nourishment not only does an area of grass give a wonderful winter colour, but it also lends itself to shaping and sculpture.

The most common mistake in lawn design occurs when an elegant green rectangle is gradually eroded by the surrounding borders, which creep into the lawn and reduce its shape to an amorphous blob. Much better to go for a bold but simple shape such as a circle, oval or square (see page 109), remembering to leave a deep flower border of at least 1m (3ft) at its narrowest point. Don't feel obliged to put the lawn in the middle of a garden with borders around it. Try designing the other way round with a border as a central feature. (See 'A Suburban Family Garden' on page 120, where the border is encompassed by two lawns.)

If you intend to lay a new lawn, lay the turf initially over an area larger than the shape you require. Once the sods have knitted together, mark out your design with spray paint and cut a good clean edge using a half-moon spade. Seed-sown lawns can be treated in the same way. However, unless you are prepared to water every day during the summer, it is better to install any lawn in spring or autumn.

Lawns as you've never seen them before. These elegant sculpted mounds are not a feature for the faint-hearted but you might consider a scaled-down version for your own plot.

Grass isn't just for lawns. Using it in smaller sections within a path can soften the hard landscape and, as long as the turf and paving are the same height, most mowers will go straight over the top of the paving. This can transform the humble concrete slab. (See 'A Suburban Family Garden' on page 120.)

In garden-design history, lawns came long before borders and patios. Enormous mounds of earth sculpted into terraces, spirals and amphitheatres were used as far back as the eighteenth century. Admittedly not many of us these days have room for an amphitheatre, but lawns take on a new dimension with simple mounds or spirals in turf (the central point of the mown meadow path in 'A Wildlife Garden' on page 136 ends in a pleasing curvaceous mound of lawn).

Chamaemelum nobile 'Treneague' (chamomile) will take the gentle footfalls required to reach this sundial centrepiece, but would not be suitable to clothe the whole path.

I would never give up my own lawn, because I love the sensual feel of walking barefoot on it, and the smell of freshly cut grass epitomizes the summer months. I could not do without it.

If mowing is your main objection, lawns do not have to be a millstone around your neck. Allowing the grass to grow and introducing native flowers and bulbs can turn your lawn into a spectacular meadow which will need to be cut only two or three times a year. Traditionally the meadow was also the place for fruit trees, providing a soft landing for falling fruit. The combination of trees and wild flowers with the addition of a mown path or two is a garden in itself.

But if you really can't face mowing even twice a year, there is an alternative for a low-use lawn. A variety of chamomile called 'Treneague' has been used for scented ornamental lawns for hundreds of years. Unlike its larger cousins, 'Treneague' grows only 10cm (4in) high and will take gentle traffic. In fact, its original use was as a surface for playing a game of bowls.

(Above) Formal brick
edges to a lawn will
help to keep the crisp
shape. Remember to
line the centrepoint of
your circle with the vista
to keep your design even.

(Right) Lock up your
lawnmower, meadows are
low-maintenance heaven.

PAVING MATERIALS

By far the greatest expense you will incur when creating your garden will be in hard landscape materials. Your choice may have to be dictated by cost, but with a little imagination even the most mundane concrete slab can become part of an interesting scheme.

Let's start with the least expensive choice, which has to be gravel. This is also one of my favourites – I love the delicious crunching sound it makes underfoot. It is versatile, and available in every colour from white through buff to almost black. There is even a variation made from crushed glass that comes in a myriad of colours and, yes, you can walk on it – I have tried it barefoot. The main advantages to gravel are that no skilled labour is needed to lay it, only a strong back, and if it is spread over a geotextile membrane it becomes the ultimate low-maintenance material. It can also be laid right up to and even underneath plants or hedges.

The combination of gravel and timber executed in perfect squares can be used as a foil for box's (*Buxus sempervirens*) formal qualities.

A good look at the materials with which your house is constructed can help you decide on the style and colour of your garden paving. It is pleasing to the eye to echo the colour of the brick or the shade of the paintwork. Try to use a maximum of only three materials in your design – any more than this and the garden can look 'bitty', unless the materials are obscured from one another within the design.

The size of paving unit can help or hinder your design. For example, a small unit like a cobble will lend

Mixing mediums such as gravel and timber gives a textural quality to your garden, which can be further enhanced by the addition of feathery grasses.

itself to curves, circles and swirls, whereas a large stone slab is useful in formal straight schemes.

Bricks are a great material to link the house to the garden. However, don't be tempted to use house bricks in a patio floor. They are not always suitable for laying on the ground and you may find that the surface shales and crumbles during the first frost. Much better to use a product designed for the job. There are lots of brick surfaces available in blue/black as well as terracotta.

FEATURES
AND STRUCTURES

You may consider objects such as seats and pergolas to be the luxury extras in your garden, but they are in fact as essential as borders and terraces. Imagine a room without furniture – that is just how your garden would feel without these types of features, so remember to choose them carefully and decorate your garden room with style.

SEATING

Within my half-acre plot I have seven places to sit and rest. It is not that I am lazy, but each one of these places is a stage where I can set a scene. When you sit to look at a garden, you immediately change the level of the view, allowing you to take in vistas or statements within the garden.

Some seating areas are only for hovering, and seating that is uncomfortable but stunning to look at can act almost like a sculpture to focus the eye.

It is possible to combine planting and seating so that the two become the same feature, such as a bower or chamomile seat. Popular in gardens from medieval times, these served two purposes: to provide privacy to courting couples as well as scent to mask unpleasant smells in the days before washing was considered routine!

Seating gives us the opportunity to introduce colour and texture into a scheme. If you desire a place to contemplate and relax, perhaps out of sight of the rest of the garden, you might require a subtle look. If this is the case, use materials that blend

The curved arms of this oak seat (above) are echoes of the garden shape. Attention to detail, as shown here, is what makes a garden design great.

(Opposite) Secluded seating, once the reserve of clandestine embraces, can provide a welcome retreat in the corner of a busy family garden.

with the planting, merging the edges between garden and seat. For example, a woven willow roof over a terracotta brick seat can create an elegant resting place.

A stroll around any garden centre will show you that seating, especially benches, can be expensive. If your budget runs to it, there is an endless array of styles and designs, from the traditional wooden Lutyens garden seat to modern metal or perspex chairs.

As with most garden design projects, seating only needs to be as expensive as you can afford. A basic bench – two tree stumps and a length of timber – is just about as inexpensive as you can get. Don't discount inside seating for use outside, either. Auction sale rooms can be a great source of interesting tables and chairs and, when treated with one of the enormous range of wood preservatives on the market, they can become all-weather items. A word of warning here: be wary of painting garden items green. It's often the obvious choice for garden furniture, but in my opinion usually looks terrible, never quite matching the surroundings. You can't compete with nature, so go for either very pale sea green or very dark black/green. From the simplest upturned log to the most ornate metalwork bench, seating is essential in every garden, no matter what your budget or plot size.

If space is at a premium, incorporate your seating in other features. The edges of raised beds, surrounding walls of water features, even a shallow flight of steps, can become an amphitheatre for a group of friends to lounge on. If you are lucky enough to have a wall within your design, utilize this for seating. We naturally stand with our backs to the wall facing outwards, so if you have little room, design seats that drop down from the wall and can be put up again as a space-saving idea.

My favourite seat in my own garden is my swing. People are amazed that I had one long before my child was even thought of.

Invest in new and innovative seating for a modern garden. You may have to stretch your budget, but in return, you might purchase a design classic.

(Opposite) Painting an ordinary bench can lift it from the realms of the mundane. Choose your colour wisely, always opting for a subtle shade, preferably one that picks up the tone of foliage or a flower.

It was made for me by my partner and has given me hours of pleasure, swinging back and forth contemplating the universe. The drawback of swings is that they need a frame, but if you don't have a tree limb large and strong enough, hang it from a pergola. An extension of the swing is the hammock, another of my favourites. This is great under a shady pergola, but if you prefer full sun, erect posts in the same way as you would fence posts and sling the hammock between them. Be sure to choose a hammock made of solid canvas, not string, or your bottom will look like a button-backed Chesterfield after you've reclined in it!

PERGOLAS

No sooner have I begun a design than I find the idea of a pergola of some sort creeping into my thoughts. It is one of the most useful garden features and especially good in a new plot when you are starting from scratch. The most common mistake I see in gardens is a lack of height. Pergolas address this, giving an instant three-dimensional look.

A pergola could be described as any type of skeletal structure, either for sitting under or walking through, made of any material and with or without plants, so really use your imagination to create a feature all your own. In fact, when two or more arches are gathered together, that's almost a pergola.

The material most commonly used for pergolas is wood; it's also one of the most versatile. The kits available are useful if you don't have the resources for a bespoke pergola, but be careful with their scale. They are often on the mean side. You need to have good head clearance, and the more chunky the uprights, the better they look. Unfortunately, as with decks, they are usually stained an unpleasant shade, so consider applying a coloured wood stain to complement your design.

(Above) This pergola may look like an umbrella in high wind, but the stark modern design is softened into its surroundings by skilful planting. Contemporary designs can be all the more acceptable if you are a clever plantsman.

(Far right) Don't feel that you have to clothe your pergola in a dozen different genus of plant – one plant repeated many times will create a bold and successful scheme.

(Right) A quality construction using oak, such as this one, will hold its own as a garden feature without intrusive planting.

Bespoke pergolas give you more room to manoeuvre, using curves with fanned joists and making a feature on a much grander scale, perhaps with a sloping roof. If you are looking for a natural feel to your pergola, perhaps something to grow a rose or honeysuckle over, oak is the best material; it will stand almost forever and weather to a beautiful silver-grey tone.

If your pergola is to run alongside your house, you could attach the pergola roof to the building, dispensing with uprights on one side. This gives the pergola a solid feel and makes the garden seem part of the house. When the doors of the house are open, the pergola feels like a transitional room between inside and outside. You might consider making the uprights of the same material as your house: brick pillars work well with a timber roof.

For a design that creates sinuous curves, make the acquaintance of your local blacksmith. Most can make any shape you desire by twisting metal rods – perhaps a steel dome for apple trees to grow over or a snaking avenue of uprights with taut wires strung between them to support climbers.

Awnings are another of my favourite features, bridging the gap between summer house and pergola. They consist simply of uprights with a canvas sail or canopy pulled taut. Their style can vary from bright-coloured Bedouin tent to contemporary asymmetric sail.

RETREATS: FOLLIES, SUMMER HOUSES, BOTHIES AND TREE HOUSES

A garden retreat can be a major financial investment. First you need to decide whether it is to be practical or a 'folly'. Perhaps you want a building that will allow you to use the garden in inclement weather, to give you another view on the garden and extra living space; or perhaps, like some of our wealthier

Who wants to live in a house? I'm moving down the garden. A summerhouse can be a simple shelter or, like this one, an extravagant fantasy. Think of it as an extra room for your house.

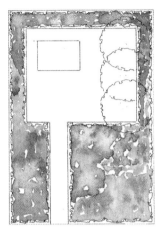

Diagram 1

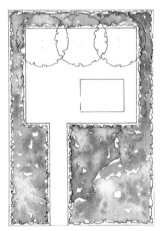

Diagram 2

(Above, top)
The summerhouse is directly in line with the path, enticing the viewer to make the journey down the garden.

(Above, bottom)
The summerhouse is hidden from initial view, to be discovered when arriving at the lawn.

ancestors, you fancy a stone 'ruin', whose sole purpose is to add beauty to the garden – apart from being a place for clandestine meetings.

If you are looking for a retreat for practical use, there are plenty of wooden styles available off the peg, though many of them look like glorified garden sheds! Should you be buying this way, go for the simplest design, with no fretwork or fancy balustrades, and consider painting the building in your own choice of colour. Most come in an unpleasant orange tone: far better to have a subtle shade of duck-egg blue or lichen grey/green. A real roof in slate, terracotta or oak shingles will help to give an elegant look.

If you are fortunate enough to have a strong, mature tree in your garden, why not put your summer house in it? Tree houses are not just for children. A structure as simple as a wooden platform with rails becomes a place of peace and retreat when nestled among the branches.

Your choice of building will also be dictated by whether your retreat is to be a feature of the garden or a secret place. Bear in mind that it will be a solid shape and can look overpowering if it is placed in the wrong spot. For example, within the design above (see Diagrams 1 and 2) the first position puts the retreat as a 'reward' at the end of the vista, whereas the second position gives the retreat a secret location, with its own part of the garden hidden from the view of the path.

OBELISKS AND SCULPTURES

Obelisks and sculptures are decorative touches that can make or break a design. They add the essential element of height that a new garden can easily lack.

Obelisks are tall slender structures constructed usually of wood or metal and occasionally of woven willow. These willow obelisks are excellent in a soft gentle scheme with either sweet peas or climbing beans growing through them. Grouped in threes, with each one a different height, they make an attractive feature. They tend not to be as tall as their formal cousins and won't last as long if left out all year round.

Wooden obelisks are my favourite and I like to use them as features in their own right without the interference of plants. Proportion is the key to success with wooden obelisks and I wouldn't shy away from making them at least 2m (6½ft), if not 3m (10ft), tall.

Without plants they are delicate and, as you can see the garden through them, they interrupt the view without blocking it out. Try siting them either side of a path or steps to give a feeling of grandeur, or down the centre of a herbaceous border. They will provide good winter interest, especially when strung with frost-sprinkled spiders' webs. To increase the impact of a box garden, a wooden obelisk placed in the central spot, especially if painted a deep red or lavender, will add colour to the scheme.

As for metal obelisks, there are some great ones on the market, especially good for growing roses over, as they are subtle enough to blend into the scheme and allow the blooms to shine. Alternatively, have them in polished steel in a contemporary design and they become a sculpture in their own right.

A stately coloured obelisk gives structural form to the border, which will last into the winter when the herbaceous plants have died down.

41

Talking of sculptures – well, I'd really rather not. Art in the garden is a difficult area. I am greatly in favour of it, but when it comes to choosing a piece I would always rather provide a plinth as part of the design and let the client select their own sculpture. One man's tasteful sculpture is another's tacky monstrosity. When it comes to siting the artwork, think about viewing it from the house. You will probably regard your sculpture as the pride and joy of your garden, so you will want to be able to see it as much as possible: the end of a vista or the centre of a circular terrace would be a good position.

URNS AND POTS

Garden containers often seem to be added as an afterthought to fill a bare spot, whereas they should be one of the integral items within a design. They do have several enormous disadvantages, however. If you intend to plant them, they will always be susceptible to drying out, so a built-in watering system is useful, otherwise you need a watering can and a great deal of self-discipline.

The supply of nutrients in the small amount of earth in a pot will eventually run out, so you will be responsible for feeding as well as watering. Terracotta containers are also susceptible to breaking in frost. Large pots tend to overbalance in the wind and you would be amazed at how many pots are stolen, even the large ones. Don't get me wrong – I am greatly in favour of containers in the garden. It's just that you need to know what you are letting yourself in for before you include

them in your design.

A container as a starting point for a design can be an exciting prospect. If you have fallen in love with an unfeasibly large urn at the garden centre, why not buy it and base your design around it, even if

Framing your favourite garden feature will give it added impact.

you have to remortgage the house to afford it! When an urn is a design feature, it needs to be at the centre of its own area, either where two or more paths converge, or at the end of a vista as a 'reward'. And don't feel the need to fill it with plants: a large urn or a pot is beautiful in its own right and doesn't need dressing.

Containers provide a way of adding extra colour to a scheme, such as in 'A Coastal Garden' on page 140. The duck-egg-blue stained deck might be a bit stark and overbearing, but the addition of soft terracotta urns brings some warmer colour and allows the planting of tender agave (these, along with their urns, will need protection from frost in winter). On a windy site, as this is assumed to be, it is a good idea to weight the bottom of your container to lower the centre of gravity and decrease the chance of it blowing over. At the other extreme, if you are using containers on a balcony or roof garden where you need to keep the weight down, fill the bottom with chunks of polystyrene instead of rock before you add your soil, so as to lighten the load.

Pots in groups, as in 'A Coastal Garden', should be arranged in odd numbers and with different heights and shapes. Play with your arrangement until it looks right, then fill the containers in situ as they can be hard to move once planted. When choosing pots, always go for ones larger than you imagine you need. If cost is an issue, have fewer containers but large ones.

The choice of materials is almost limitless. If you want a formal scheme, a square container, such as the lead tank in 'A Garden for the Senses' on page 132, will add majesty and order. If lead is too expensive, square wooden containers will do. These square planters are often called Versailles tubs.

The urns in 'A Garden for the Disabled', on page 144, are a real show-stopper. Chest-height and made of sandstone, they form the type of centrepiece that I describe above. A smaller urn on a tall plinth would have the same effect.

Don't discount containers in some of the more contemporary materials. Cast concrete, stainless steel and even glass blocks can all be successful. In my garden I have old galvanized watering cans and florists' buckets filled with grasses and bulbs.

If you intend to plant your container, try to get away from the awful multi-coloured annual explosions that have always been so popular. Almost any type of plant, from oak trees to snowdrops, is suitable for container planting, and don't feel obligated to mix your genera. A single type of plant in a large container has a great deal more impact than a mixture.

Remember

🌿 Select your pot, then buy the next size up.

🌿 Choose a material that either adds an accent colour or blends with the scheme.

🌿 Group pots in odd numbers – unless they are either side of a path, when two are best.

🌿 You are responsible for providing water and food.

(Opposite) Try to resist the urge to plant anything that will hold compost. Allow a pot such as this to exist on its own and work on complementary planting around it.

BOUNDARIES

B y 'boundaries' I don't mean the ones we are pushing forward in the field of garden design but the ones that separate you from the rest of the world. If you are fortunate enough to look out over pastoral magnificence, you may wish to skip this chapter. However, if, as for most people, your view is next door's drying smalls, read on.

Very few of us have so little tolerance that we end up in raging disputes over boundaries. Negotiation and communication are the key to success. You cannot put up a boundary fence more than 2m (6½ft) from ground level without the permission of both owners and planning consent from the local council. If you remove any foliage or branches from trees that belong to your neighbour, but overhang your property, you must offer to return the cut branches. Technically they are your neighbour's property. Contrary to popular belief, in Britain there is no such thing as right of light. If your neighbour's trees are huge and turn your garden into a black hole, your only line of attack is negotiation.

As well as keeping out the world, boundaries provide a backdrop or foil for your design. What is behind a feature can make or break it. If you want something to stand out, the backdrop should be of a contrasting colour or material: for example, a pale stone urn looks good in front of a deep green yew hedge, or a purple *Phormium* in front of a cream wall. However, if you choose to have a bold-coloured boundary, make sure that you

(Above) A traditional weather-worn picket fence provides a separating line for the garden without eliminating the view.

(Opposite) The entrance to your garden sets the scene for the arriving viewer. You just know that a grand gateway such as this is going to lead to a beautiful garden.

continue the theme into the rest of the garden by picking up the colour or material in other features, otherwise the boundary will look odd and out of place. Without balance a design feature can eclipse everything else in the garden, drawing too much attention to itself.

Natural materials, such as reed, bamboo, wood and willow, have a more subtle look to finish your design. They can act as a frame for climbing plants, providing support without eclipsing the beauty of the flowers. If you are looking for a budget fence, a simple post-and-wire structure is sufficient to define your boundary and, once covered in greenery, such as *Hedera helix* (ivy), can itself be a striking feature.

It is worth noting that the usual option taken for fencing is not only expensive but also very ugly: my pet boundary hate, orange larch-lap fencing. If you are already in possession of this product, never fear – it will fade eventually. However, more pleasing would be to paint it or, if you don't want to introduce colour, stain the wood a darker shade. While a dark wood-toned stain will be suitable for a natural look, there are plenty of coloured wood stains to choose from. A shade of dark blue will cover the orange and leave a striking background to the garden. Go for a deep subtle shade: if you choose too bright a tone, the fence will shout 'BLUE' at you when you walk into the garden. Try to come to an agreement with your neighbour about the colour of your fence, even if it is legally yours. It is very hard to colour one side of a fence without the paint dripping down the other.

The height of your boundary will be dictated by what you want to see over it. If you have something beautiful to look at outside your property, keep the fence low and use the view. This is known as borrowed landscape. If you are fortunate enough to have a picturesque view beyond your boundary, or a

(Above) If you want to use a really bold colour on your boundary, like this cobalt blue, don't forget to echo the colour in other features such as the seat and obelisk. This will give the garden unity and won't make the fence stand out like a sore thumb.

(Far right) *Hedera helix* (ivy) is the greatest utility plant as it will cling unsupported to any fence or wall, providing you with a solid green foil or hiding any number of sins.

(Right) Cute cottage planting is given a defining line by the use of a traditional picket fence. I am not sure if the fence is keeping the garden in, or out.

beautiful feature such as a church spire or copse of trees, try to incorporate it into your design. You can do this by arranging a vista within the garden to point the viewer towards the feature, or simply by cutting a window in the boundary to give a framed picture to look out on. If the surrounding landscape comes right to your property, you do not have to put up any kind of boundary, unless your house deeds require it. Just let the landscape run into your design.

Boundaries can also provide shelter for the garden, but do not make the common mistake of expecting a tall fence to be the solution. If you live in a particularly windy area, such as on the coast, do not erect a 2m (6½ft) solid wooden fence. It will last about one season before you wake up one morning to find it in the next county. With a solid boundary the wind will hit one side and rush over the top in a channelled force, creating an eddy, so not only will the fence fall over but you will create small hurricanes on your side of the boundary. A far better solution is to create a permeable barrier that allows the wind to pass through while slowing it down. Depending on the fierceness of your conditions, hedging is perfect for this and, if room allows, a copse of native trees will also help interrupt the flow. Alternatively willow hurdles, post-and-rail and hit-and-miss fences all allow the elements through while lessening their harsh effects. If you want privacy, then a hit-and-miss fence is ideal. It looks like a solid fence, but in actual fact the boards are placed on alternate sides of the horizontal rails, which allows gusts of wind to pass through.

Similarly designed fencing can be used to combat the invasion of noise pollution. Rigid boundaries such as solid fences or walls can just accentuate the problem, bouncing the sound round and round, unless you combine them with lots of

Should you be lucky enough not to want to screen out the rest of the world, you could opt for a delicate fence that allows a view beyond your own garden.

vegetation to absorb the noise. Think how a room with no furniture accentuates sound: that is just about how your fenced garden will sound without plants.

If you are unfortunate enough to have an eyesore at the end of your garden or even next door, you might feel like erecting the tallest fence possible and then adding trellis and plants – just about anything to hide the view – but unfortunately this often creates exactly the opposite effect. It's rather like growing a beautiful climber over an ugly shed: all you achieve is to draw the eye towards the nasty feature, not away from it.

You would do better to put up a medium-sized fence in a dark colour, which will recede into the background, and then make a great feature at the point farthest away from your eyesore, thus drawing the viewer's attention to better things. If you must go for a cover-up, a tree or three will help, but remember that, as you move around the garden, the ugly feature will become visible from another vantage point and you may find you need an entire wood to hide it.

Next to hedges, with their disadvantage of needing time to mature, my favourite boundary is a wall. This enables you to echo the material of your house in the construction and give continuity to the garden. Brick and stone are relatively expensive materials to use, but remember that you are creating a feature that will stand for a long time and will need no maintenance. However, there are less expensive ways to build a wall using block and render and, while natural beige render can be left unfinished, it is also possible to paint the surface to enhance your design.

Walls offer the opportunity to incorporate other interesting features. For a start they don't have to be straight. Providing your neighbour agrees, you could build a 'crinkle-crankle' wall, which looks charming and provides recesses for fruit trees, statues or a seat. Mirrors incorporated into an archway in a wall fool the viewer into believing there is more to your garden and can also reflect light into a dark corner. Set mirrors as decoration along a line, as in 'A Stylish Minimal Garden' on page 116. If you don't want to use mirrors, a false doorway consisting of an old wooden door set in a frame and fixed to a wall will give the impression of a large garden, even if the door doesn't actually lead anywhere.

Whatever type of wall you decide on, always employ a professional builder to do the job for you and make sure you have a coping stone on the top of the wall or you may find that it suffers from damp problems.

A crinkle-crankle wall will need twice as many bricks as an ordinary straight one, not to mention a great deal more planning. But it will provide the ultimate area for growing espalier fruits and be something of a talking point.

A gate is your opportunity to entice the visitor in. Use it to give a hint of the delights to come.

GATES

Many gardens are reached solely by access through the house. This raises lots of problems when you are trying to bring construction materials into the garden. If your neighbours have road access to their plot, try to negotiate temporary access across their land by removing one of your party-fence panels for the duration of your build. However, if you are lucky enough to have access through a boundary gate, not only will you avoid compost on the carpet but you have another design opportunity. The gate will probably be the first impression that the visitor gets of your garden. It should echo the theme of the garden and draw the visitor in. Repeating the material and style of the boundary fence is a good start. Make sure that the gate is either exactly the same height as the fence or a completely different height. This is not as stupid as it sounds: if the gate is a centimetre or two above or below the fence, it looks unprofessional, so try to make it either a definite match or a contrasting height. It is also wise to allow a good gap at the

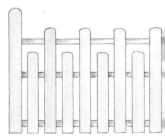

If there are fantastic views beyond your garden, even if you don't own them, you can pretend by borrowing them. Placing a gate with a view beyond will appear to lead to the 'rest' of your garden.

bottom of the gate to allow water to flow underneath in heavy rain.

Enough of the practicalities – gates can be fun. Play with the perspective of your entrance. A small gate with an arch overhead, so that you have to stoop to enter, gives a magical *Alice in Wonderland* feel; alternatively go for a double-gate grand entrance for a feeling of majesty and importance.

HEDGES

Between 1760 and 1860 the British Parliament created the Enclosure Acts. These ordered the division of England into separate parcels and decreed that each area should be divided by hedges. Today, when it comes to separating your garden from the rest of the world, the usual solution is a fence. Hedges are much less favoured for two reasons: they take time to mature enough to give a solid barrier of sizeable height and they need to be tended regularly to maintain order.

Personally, I would always favour a hedge over a fence when the design allows, for one very good reason – a hedge can be far less expensive than the cheapest fence. If you plant a single line of native species during the bare-root season of October/November to March/April, your hedge will cost you a fraction of the pot-grown price. Plants like *Crataegus* (hawthorn) and *Fagus* (beech) mixed with a little *Ilex* (holly) will create a hedge that, along with harbouring all sorts of wildlife from bugs to birds, becomes a calendar of the year. You will get blossom in the spring, a dense green wall in the summer, a tapestry of green and bronze foliage in autumn and scarlet berries in the winter.

(Opposite) Use yew hedging to create a majestic feel. These gigantic 3-metre hedges channel you around the garden, insisting on which direction you walk.

Hedge planting and maintenance

PLANT	DISTANCE	CLIPPING TIME
Crataegus monogyna (hawthorn)	30cm (1ft) apart	Trim twice from early summer to autumn
Fagus sylvatica (beech)	50cm (20in) apart	Clip once in mid-summer
Ilex aquifolium (holly)	50cm (20in) apart	Clip once in mid-summer
Ligustrum ovalifolium (privet)	40cm (15in) apart	Trim during summer as necessary Don't allow to get too woody
Taxus baccata (yew)	50cm (20in) apart	Clip once in late summer

If this sounds appealing but you just can't wait for the plants to grow, consider an inexpensive fence, possibly using second-hand panels, with a hedge planted just in front. The fence has to last only a few seasons, then you can get rid of it, by which time the hedge will be romping away.

Perhaps native hedging is too informal and rural-looking for your design. *Taxus baccata* (yew) may be more to your taste. Famed for its poisonous berries and inclusion in churchyards, it is the finest dense hedge you can have. In anything but the wettest ground it lends itself readily to sculpting into alcoves and buttresses or an ornamental castellated top; and, if you already have a yew hedge that is out of hand, you can cut it back at will, as it has the most marvellous regenerative properties, shooting fresh branches out from the main stem.

An adaptation of the willow fence is to use the willow live, creating a boundary that is a hybrid between a fence and a hedge. The whips can be planted in long lengths, which will

Hedges needn't run as straight lines; use them like this beech (*Fagus sylvatica*) to make sculptural, maze-like curves.

provide instant privacy, and then gently woven in and out of one another to make a tactile lattice. Although this is a traditional rural craft, the resulting sculptural hedges can look great in any style of garden, even very contemporary ones. The incorporation of metal hoops and contorted shapes gives them a surreal look.

Lastly, don't overlook the use of hedges within a garden. The division of a garden space into compartments can add interest to a large open area and mystery to a smaller plot. While you might wish to prevent the viewer from seeing the whole of your garden at once, the use of a small window cut into the dividing hedges, known as fenestration, will offer tantalizing glimpses of what is yet to be discovered.

These beautiful mounded hedges are sensual and tactile. They guide the way to the rest of the garden and look as if they might envelop you.

WATER

I wish I could think of a better analogy than to call a water feature the beating heart of a garden, but I really can't, because that is exactly what it is. Water is life-giving, always alive with wildlife, bestowing motion, sound and visual beauty on a design. In a garden it is often the central feature on which the rest of the design will hang.

In my own garden a land drain runs from the field at the end through our plot and out under the adjoining car park. A land drain might not sound glamorous or inspiring, but it provides a stream of rainwater collected from the field, and although it flows only after rain, that merely adds to its idiosyncrasy. A garden design relies on capitalizing on a plot's natural features, such as aspect, slope or environmental conditions, but if you are lucky enough to have a natural flow of water, even if it is just a land drain, you need to incorporate it into your design.

A stream or spring will breathe life into your garden; however, don't feel that if you have a natural stream you are limited to only a naturalistic style of garden. Water tumbling over craggy rocks will suit some designs, but you can just as easily channel the water along a formal canal or rill. Always be careful when dealing with natural water courses: they have a constantly changing flow, depending on the weather conditions, so your feature will have to allow for this. If you want to run your stream into a pond, make sure that there is an exit for the water, to return it to its original course.

(Above) An exciting water feature. Three-metre water jets spout from a granite base.

(Opposite) The epitome of perfect reflection in a still canal, with a tantalising glimpse of the landscape beyond.

When the land drain in my garden isn't running I can still satisfy my thirst for a water feature with my static one. This is just about the most simple water feature that you could have and it goes to prove that they need not be complicated or expensive. I rescued a galvanized tank about 80cm (2½ ft) square from a local tip. Sunk flush with the ground in the centre of a chamomile lawn, it is filled with water and white pigmy water lilies. It is an elegant, understated feature, full of waxy blooms and flurries of dragonflies.

A natural scheme – a pond of static water surrounded by natural planting – can provide a calm and tranquil oasis. Perhaps you may be put off this type of feature for fear of the water becoming stagnant, but there are ways to ensure that it stays fresh. Oxygenating plants are a great help, together with fish and the natural supply of rain water, and, in a formal pond, there are chemicals that you can add to clear it of unwanted organisms.

The only downside of planting a static water feature is that you can lose the wonderful reflective qualities of still water. You will get some small reflection of the overhanging plants but, if you want to exploit the reflections to their full potential, a simple straight-sided pond in a formal scheme will be perfect. In garden design this is referred to as a canal.

The most common and most useful type of moving water feature is known as a recycling feature. This uses the same body of water pumped from a reservoir through the feature and allowed to flow back to the reservoir. Apart from the occasional top-up in the summer months, when some water will be lost due to evaporation, the system needs no additional water supply, a plus point when most homes have water meters. This type of feature requires a water pump, run on either solar

Planting around a water feature creates most impact when the plants are allowed to flow in huge unkempt drifts of one genus, such as here with this *Primula florindae*.

(Opposite) Creating a water feature that looks as natural as this one is a Herculean task. Use plants to soften the edges and hide the man-made materials. Don't miss out on the opportunity to introduce all levels of moisture-loving plants which are best-suited to this type of feature.

power or from an electrical supply. Needless to say, the electrical supply must be fitted by a qualified electrician, using a special outdoor cable. Don't try to do it yourself. Choosing the right pump for your feature can seem daunting. There are no set formulae to make this easy. The best course of action is to take a sketch of the feature, showing rough measurements and the height to which the water will travel, to your local water garden centre, where you will get professional advice on buying the correct pump.

Once you have decided which type of feature you would like to incorporate into your garden – formal or informal, static or flowing – then you can begin to design it. There are a few basic types to think about. Remember that you can mix two or more features together, and anything can make a water feature, just as long as it holds water.

BUBBLE FOUNTAIN

A bubble fountain requires only a small pump and reservoir. There is no visible standing water as it is all contained in the underground reservoir. Above ground the water appears from between stones, or through a hole drilled in a central stone, and cascades over the surrounding pebbles. This type of feature is therefore good for a small garden or a children's garden and is best used as a central feature with access on all sides. For variation you could try using coloured glass balls instead of rocks or pebbles or, for a minimalist scheme, a clear glass ball and crushed glass gravel.

FOUNTAIN

A versatile feature to fit in any style of design, a fountain uses a pond as its reservoir, the water being channelled by a pump

(Above) A rill can be a
dominant water feature
running the entire length
of your garden – although
in reality it is so narrow
that it only takes up a
fraction of space.
The simple slab bridges
allow access across the
water, although the rill
is only one stride wide.

(Far right) Any hollow
object can be used to
channel water; these
chunky bamboo poles
would work extremely
well in a contemporary
oriental setting.

(Right) If you have gone
to the trouble of creating
an elaborate moving
water feature, give it
a starring role in your
garden scheme.
This fountain is glimpsed
from every corner through
apertures in hedges
and fences.

through a jet that shoots it into the air. There are myriad nozzles available for your pump that can give effects from a single foaming column to a layered cascade. The height that you want your fountain to achieve will have a bearing on the diameter of your pond: the taller the jet, the wider the pond, as any water that is lost through splash will mean that the reservoir will drop below its required level and will need topping up more regularly. This type of feature can work as a centrepiece to a design or equally well as a 'reward' at the end of a pathway or where two pathways cross.

RILL

A rill is a small stream of solid construction that can run either at ground level or along the top of a dwarf wall. It will need a change in levels to màke it flow correctly, although this need only be slight. At the end of the rill the water will run into a reservoir that can either be hidden or can take the form of a pond as part of the feature. The water is then pumped back up to the start of the rill. This sort of feature usually works best in a controlled or formal design, around a terrace or alongside a path. The hard surface of the rill is particularly important visually. Slate looks beautiful when wet; or perhaps a ceramic mosaic of jewel-like colours to complement your planting scheme?

Use water to mask noise pollution. The tone will reduce, if not mask, the intrusive sounds. A small waterfall like this one will produce a range of sounds, depending on the depth of the water in the receiving pond.

This narrow water rill (opposite) provides a glimpse of reflection of the bright yellow bothy, and the symmetrical *Agapanthus* planting entices one to investigate.

POND

When asked to visualize a pond, most people think first of a natural shape, constructed of liner and rocks. This is not as easy to get right as you might think. Never, never leave any liner showing – it always looks awful. Ensure that the rocks or pebbles completely cover any liner that is above the water surface, and when laying rocks make sure the strata all run the same way or it will look as though you have just emptied a lorry-load of stone into the garden. Soften the edges with planting and try to get foliage at different levels, between the rocks and into the water's edge. This type of pond is appropriate for an informal and natural scheme. It's a must for any wildlife garden, but needs siting carefully. Try to get it to nestle in the design and beware of too many overhanging trees as the falling leaves in autumn can cause problems. As they rot they produce gases that are poisonous to fish.

Not many of us will have the space to do this type of pond justice. However, there are many more interesting possibilities. A pond is just a reservoir of water, so anything that is watertight has the potential to be a water feature. Reclamation yards house a treasure trove of containers, from stone troughs to galvanized tanks. There is no reason to have only one pond in your design. How about one tank set higher than another, with the water draining from the upper to the lower and a pump to return the water to the top tank? Or a tank with a water source above it, such as a wall spout? Don't just think of a lion's head with a traditional look. The water can come from copper tubes, terra-cotta pipes or hollow bamboo canes. Now we are in territory that is hard to define: is it a fountain, a pond or a bubble? Does it really matter what we call it? Just try to look at raw materials in a new light and move water between them in any way you like.

One of the simplest methods of holding water is to build a raised tank – an especially good idea if you don't like digging. It can be constructed of any material that will suit your design, or cast in concrete and painted. It might be best to get a professional to handle this type of construction as water is heavy stuff and the tank must be very strong to contain it. Once you have your feature, you can add anything you like, from a fountain to an overflowing urn to water plants. On the next page are a few planting gems you might want to consider for your water feature – including plants for every level of wetness.

Pure white *Nymphaea alba* seems to add light to a still reflective pond.

Water plants: planting list

Having water in your garden design will give you the opportunity to use plants that would otherwise be out of bounds. Here are my favourites, from floating to very damp conditions.

Bog plants
Growing conditions: damp but not drowning. Wet soil rather than permanent moisture.

Cimicifuga racemosa (bugbane)	1.5m (5ft) perennial with lovely lance-shaped leaves and white flowers in mid-summer.
Gunnera manicata (Chile rhubarb)	See page 76.
Iris sibirica (Siberian flag)	1m (3ft) tall with blue/purple blooms from spring to summer.
Primula florindae (giant yellow cowslip)	Yellow primula up to 80cm (2½ft) tall.
Schoenoplectus lacustris subsp. *tabernaemontani* 'Zebrinus'	1.5m (5ft) evergreen sedge with amazing neon striped stems.
Trollius europaeus (globeflower)	60cm (2ft) perennial producing bold yellow blooms in spring.

Water plants
Growing conditions: floating in water. Will die if allowed to dry out.

Callitriche palustris (water starwort)	Oxygenating.
Ceratophyllum demersum (hornwort)	Deciduous perennial with dark green leaves used for oxygenating.
Nymphaea alba (water lily)	Floating, dark green leaves; pure white blooms with yellow centres.

Marginal plants
Growing conditions: permanent moisture. They sit at the margins of the pond, dipping their toes in the water, but will tolerate the odd period of drying out.

Cyperus involucratus (Nile grass)	1m (3ft) evergreen sedge shiny spiky leaves with green/white flower spikes in summer.
Dierama pendulum (angel's fishing rods)	1.5m (5ft) delicate arching stems dripping with pink bells.
Matteuccia struthiopteris (ostrich fern)	1m (3ft) deciduous lush green fern.
Mentha aquatica (watermint)	1m (3ft) high with the look of an ordinary garden mint. Woolly leaves and mauve flowers.
Myosotis scorpioides (water forget-me-not)	15cm (6in) perennial with small green leaves and delicate forget-me-not flowers.
Zantedeschia aethiopica 'Crowborough' (arum lily or trumpet lily)	50cm-1m (20in–3ft), lush dark green leaves with bold white lily-like flowers in mid-summer.

WATER FOR CHILDREN

Most families with children who are planning a garden would throw their arms up in horror at the very mention of using a water feature in the design. Stories of children drowning in only a few centimetres of water are enough to frighten any parent. The truth is that water features are dangerous for very small children, but they do love them. Like grown-ups they are drawn to the sparkle, sound and motion of water. Toddlers will stare mesmerized into a moving stream.

If you want a water feature and you have children, you need to design cleverly. Bubble fountains are perfect for little hands to play in as long as the reservoir underneath is sturdily built, with a good strong metal grid that can be locked securely in place, not just resting with stones on top.

Giant majestic leaves of *Gunnera manicata* will tower at least two metres over your head with heavily-thorned stems, these prehistoric monsters are not for small gardens.

A small rill or trickle of a stream for sailing small paper boats will provide hours of entertainment – though I would not advise this type of feature for children under about four years old, just to be on the safe side. The flow need only be a centimetre or two deep to make the feature work and the addition of a bridge constructed from a single slab of stone will offer the opportunity for the endlessly amusing game of 'Pooh Sticks'.

Iris sibirica (Siberian iris) is a stalwart of moist planting, providing these vivid blooms from spring through summer. You may find they become a horticultural vandal, invading your garden, so police them carefully.

As far as children are concerned, the more water, the better, and a water feature that is a cross between a sprinkler system and a fountain is safe and will be the summer's most popular toy. One or more very fine jets of water that appear to spout straight from a paved area in a random manner can seem very exciting. The water can then drain off the cambered paving into a concealed reservoir to be used again. There are systems available that will activate these fountains by the touch of a button or, better still, are voice-activated, giving you more water the more you scream.

If your garden already includes a pond and you would like to keep it, or you really want deep water in your new design, it is possible to do this safely. You will need a strong metal grid laid over the water and secured all around the edge. Set at water level, it can be made to blend into the design and even become an essential part of the feature like the steel waves in 'A Stylish Minimal Garden' on page 116.

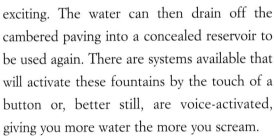

(Opposite) *Zantedeschia aethiopica* 'Crowborough'. Stately white lilies that look almost as if made from wax, they will grow equally well on the margins of the pond or in a container if well-watered.

However, if you have any doubts about using water in a garden for children, don't do it. Choose another type of feature.

DESIGNING
WITH PLANTS

C an a garden be a garden if it doesn't have plants? I would say no. Even the most minimal of spaces merits one or two striking specimen plants. While the importance of landscaping in a garden cannot be underestimated, it is a static feature. The planting scheme, however, gives the garden its spirit and personality.

It is important that gardeners do not become slaves to their gardens. Getting the right balance between the time you have available to maintain your plot and achieving the look you require is a delicate business. The practicalities of a herbaceous border, for instance, are work, work and more work. Only the very dedicated can do justice to the wide sweep of flowers that require watering, staking, deadheading, weeding, dividing and so on, though few can deny that the results are worth the effort. The downside of this type of planting is the almost total lack of visual interest in winter, save for a few seed-heads. Unless you are determined to create a true herbaceous border it is advisable to include some sedate and structured shrubs, which will not only provide you with winter interest, but will also act as foils in front of which you can display your blooms.

My grandfather would tell me that nature mixes every colour, so we can too. I am not sure that he was right. I favour planting schemes that are colour co-ordinated, a technique shown to perfection in the famous White Garden at

(Above) The foliage of this vine, *Vitis vinifera*, turns flame orange and red in the autumn, giving another dimension to its range of colours.

(Opposite) *Lilium* 'Casa Blanca', lilies are a sign of purity. They are best grown in terracotta pots and then dropped into place in a border when they are about to burst into bloom.

Sissinghurst in Kent. The planting skill and visual impact of this scheme are undeniable, but learn to look carefully at your blooms. Some shocking-pink flowers, for example, have an almost blue hue to them, so mixing them with blues will tone down the shock value and create a beautiful blend. A single-colour theme, such as lavender, will have better depth if you use plants that range from pale pink and lavender through purple to deep blue.

The hardest trick to master in planting plans is the succession from one flower to the next throughout the year. It almost requires planting one plant on top of another, so that as one bloom fades another takes over. For example, in a white and blue colour scheme, a border of 1x3m (3x10ft) might contain the collection of bulbs, perennials and good evergreen shrub listed below, which will ensure that there is an item of interest in every month of the year.

Quantities of plants can also be hard to judge, too few leaving bare earth and too many resulting in their being packed so tightly that they become leggy and straggly. Start by aiming for approximately five plants per square metre for perennials and one per square metre for shrubs or specimens. Always try

Plants for succession planting

FEATURE TIME	PLANT	NO. OF PLANTS
Jan to Feb	*Galanthus nivalis* (snowdrop)	30
Mar to Apr	*Tulipa* 'Spring Green' (tulip)	30
May to June	*Alchemilla mollis* (lady's mantle)	5
July to Aug	*Agapanthus* 'Dorothy Palmer' (agapanthus)	5
Sept to Oct	*Anemone* x *hybrida* 'Honorine Jobert' (Japanese anemone)	5
Nov to Dec (also flowers in June)	*Ceanothus* (Californian lilac)	1

to group in odd numbers – one, three, five or seven – as this has a more pleasing effect. When plants are grouped in even numbers, the brain tends to divide them into their individual units, whereas odd numbers become one amorphous drift.

Although this chaotic border scheme may look as if it has grown together by accident, that is just a testament to the skill of the plantsman. Shades of pink and yellow have been carefully combined with highlights of bold blue.

PLANTS I CAN'T DESIGN WITHOUT:
BEST PERFORMERS AND HARDEST WORKERS

I could fill a book twice this size with planting plans and plant combinations. The possible variations based on just one individual's taste in colour and style are mind-boggling; when you add the variables of conditions, climate and orientation, these become infinite. So I am only going to guide you in this area. The plants in the lists on the following pages are the ones that reappear time and again within my designs. In general they are not rare, hard to source or difficult to grow, but they bring

Foliage plants

Name	Type	Feature/uses	Condition	Height	At their best
Alchemilla mollis (lady's mantle)	Perennial	Fills in the gaps in beds with vibrant lime flowers. Very free-seeding.	Any	60cm (2ft)	Summer
Buxus sempervirens (box)	Evergreen shrub	Great hedges or, if left loose in a border, will provide a good backbone. Classic plant for topiary.	Any	2m (6½ft)	All year
Eucalyptus pauciflora subsp. *niphophila* (eucalyptus)	Evergreen shrub	Soft blue/grey leaves on arching branches.	Sun Good to pollard or coppice.	10m (33ft)	All year
Foeniculum vulgare 'Purpureum' (bronze fennel)	Perennial	Bronze feathery foliage, good foil.	Sun	2m (6½ft)	Spring, summer, autumn
Gunnera manicata	Perennial	Prehistoric-looking monster for moist areas such as pond margins.	Sun/semi-shade	2m (6½ft)	Spring, summer, autumn
Hedera helix (ivy)	Evergreen climber	Good cover for ground or building; mix with clematis if you want flowers and foliage.	Semi-shade	4m (13ft)	All year
Humulus lupulus 'Aureus' (golden hop)	Perennial climber	Bright lime leaves will cover pergola in one season with heavy boughs of hops in late summer.	Sun	6m (20ft)	Spring, summer, autumn
Pittosporum tenuifolium	Evergreen shrub	Shiny-leaved shrub for the backbone of a border.	Any	4m (13ft)	All year
Polygonatum × hybridum (Solomon's seal)	Perennial	Foliage plant for shady forest floor.	Semi-shade	1m (3ft)	Early summer
Rosmarinus officinalis (rosemary)	Evergreen shrub	Knockout scent with delicate mauve or blue flowers. Practical and pretty.	Sun/semi-shade	1.5m (5ft)	All year
Salvia officinalis 'Purpurascens' (purple sage)	Evergreen shrub	Purple/green young foliage with purple flowers. Great in a blue border scheme.	Sun/semi-shade	60cm (2ft)	All year
Soleirolia soleirolii (mind-your-own-business)	Evergreen perennial	Carpet of vivid green tiny leaves with an insatiable appetite for space.	Sun/semi-shade	5cm (2in)	All year
Taxus baccata (yew)	Evergreen tree	Solid hedge or feature tree in ground that is not too moist.	Any	10m (33ft)	All year
Vitis vinisfera (vine)	Deciduous climber	Spectacular bronze foliage for pergola coverage.	Sun/semi-shade	7m (23ft)	Spring, summer autumn

Eucalyptus pauciflora subsp. *niphophila*

Humulus lupulus 'Aureus'

Hedera helix

(Opposite) *Polygonatum × hybridum* (Solomon's seal).

Flowers

Name	Type	Feature/uses	Condition	Height	At their best
Agapanthus 'Dorothy Palmer'	Perennial	Fabulous in pots or large clumps in border; bold fireworks on sturdy stems.	Sun	75cm (2½ft)	Late summer
Allium cristophii	Summer bulb	Drop-dead gorgeous, at least fifty delicate pink/purple flowers on one round head.	Sun	40cm (15in)	Summer
Anemone × *hybrida* 'Honorine Jobert'	Perennial	Late summer white flowers when so many others are fading.	Semi-shade	1.5m (5ft)	Late summer
Clematis armandii (virgin's bower)	Deciduous climber	A great grower; masses of white scented flowers for a south wall.	Sun	5m (16ft)	Spring
Digitalis purpurea (foxglove)	Biennial	For border or woodland; the ultimate cottage-style bloom.	Semi-shade	1.5m (5ft)	Early summer
Eremurus himalaicus (foxtail lily)	Perennial	Tall dense racemes of white flowers; real impact for the border.	Sun/semi-shade	2.5m (8ft)	Summer
Fritillaria meleagris (snake's head fritillary)	Spring bulb	Heart-wrenching beauty, small nodding heads of chequer-board design.	Sun/semi-shade	30cm (1ft)	Spring
Galanthus nivalis (snowdrop)	Spring bulb	The first joy of the year, best in drifts in the lawn.	Semi-shade	15cm (6in)	Spring
Helleborus niger (Christmas rose)	Perennial	First white border flowers of the year, great for cutting.	Semi-shade	45cm (1½ft)	Spring
Lavandula angustifolia 'Hidcote' (lavender)	Evergreen shrub	Hedge with scent, or striking as part of a border.	Sun	60cm (2ft)	Summer
Lilium 'Casa Blanca' (lily)	Summer bulb	Pure white breathtaking bloom with blinding scent. Fabulous in pots.	Sun	60cm (2ft)	Summer
Liriope muscari	Evergreen perennial	Great ground cover. Spiky leaves and lovely mauve spikes of flowers.	Semi-shade	30cm (1ft)	Autumn
Perovskia atriplicifolia 'Blue Spire' (Russian sage)	Sub-shrub	Profusion of lavender-blue spires over scented grey foliage.	Sun	1m (3ft)	Late summer
Philadelphus 'Virginal' (mock orange blossom)	Deciduous shrub	Scented centrepiece for border.	Sun/semi-shade	2m (6½ft)	Mid-summer
Pratia pedunculata	Evergreen perennial	Creeping mass of tiny leaves, producing pale blue star-shaped flowers. Likes moisture.	Semi-shade	1m (3ft)	Summer
Rosa 'Korhassi' (compass rose)	Deciduous shrub	White blooms and scent for a border or loose hedge.	Sun/semi-shade	1.5m (5ft)	Summer
Verbascum × *phoeniceum* 'Gainsborough'	Perennial	Lemon flower on spires with a lovely downy nest of leaves.	Sun	1m (3ft)	Early summer
Viola tricolor (heartsease)	Short-lived perennial	Self-seeding vandal with delicate flowers in combinations of yellow, purple and lavender.	Sun	15cm (6in)	Spring, summer, autumn

(Above) *Verbascum* ×
phoeniceum
'Gainsborough'.

(Far right) *Viola tricolor*
(heartsease).

(Right) *Allium cristophii.*

Feature plants

Name	Type	Feature/uses	Condition	Height	At their best
Angelica archangelica (angelica)	Perennial	Bright green foliage with firework-style lime-green heads.	Sun	2m (6½ft)	Summer
Cedrus deodara	Evergreen tree	Feature tree; drama queen.	Semi-shade	20m (65ft)	All year
Corylus avellana 'Contorta' (twisted hazel)	Deciduous shrub	Statement plant or bulk for a bed. Fabulous silhouette and catkins in spring.	Sun/semi-shade	5m (16ft)	All year
Cynara cardunculus (cardoon)	Perennial	Massive downy silver-green leaves giving rise to gigantic purple thistles.	Sun	2m (6½ft)	Summer
Fagus sylvatica 'Dawyck' (beech)	Deciduous tree	Erect, sentinel-style columnar tree.	Sun/semi-shade	7m (23ft)	Summer
Garrya elliptica (silk-tassel bush)	Evergreen shrub	Happy to lean against walls. Hard waxy leaves with long pale green/grey catkins in winter.	Sun/semi-shade	2m (6½ft)	Winter
Juniperus scopulorum 'Skyrocket'	Evergreen tree	Elegant narrow tree in a glaucous blue tone. Lives up to its name.	Sun/semi-shade	8m (26ft)	All year
Liriodendron tulipifera (tulip tree)	Deciduous tree	Feature plant with fabulous flowers; bit of a talking point.	Sun/semi-shade	30m (100ft)	Summer
Ophiopogon planiscapus 'Nigrescens'	Evergreen	Great edging plant or feature in pots.	Sun/semi-shade	30cm (1ft)	All year
Phormium tenax	Evergreen	Showy plant with sword-shaped upright leaves.	Sun/semi-shade	2m (6½ft)	All year

Corylus avellana 'Contorta'

Liriodendron tulipifera

Garrya elliptica

(Opposite) *Ophiopogon planiscapus* 'Nigrescens'.

foliage, flower and form to my schemes, each one being hard-working in its own way. Use these as a basis for further investigation or as 'top-ups' for an existing border scheme.

As a rule you should always try to locate a plant in an area that will give it the ideal conditions for growth. However, I am frequently told how well plants do when placed in a position not thought suitable, so if you really want to grow a particular plant, just have a go. It might work. Most likely it will merely survive, whereas what we want for our plants is that they thrive. A common problem is that one plant will grow better than others, increasing in size and eclipsing its neighbours. Take care over your planting and police them strictly. You are in charge of your plants, not the other way round.

If a design begs for tender plants, I will succumb to the temptation, but in general I prefer plants that can survive a snowy winter. Therefore all the plants in my list are hardy. They also do not need either acidic or alkaline conditions but prefer neutral, and will tolerate a little of both.

When your garden design outline is finished, the most exciting part of the process begins. The planting schemes in your garden will make or break it. Get this wrong and you can ruin a good design. Get it right and you can elevate a mediocre garden to the realms of excellence.

So how do you begin? You need to ensure that the selection of plants provides interest throughout every season. That does not necessarily mean flower. The use of structural plants for their outstanding berries, stems or foliage cannot be under-estimated. The basic formula is to start with a few plants to provide the backbone to your border. These fall into either the 'foliage' or 'feature' category. Their main job is to provide all-year-round density to the scheme. They should be evergreen or

(Above) *Fritillaria meleagris* (snake's head fritillary).

(Far right) *Helleborus niger* (hellebore).

(Right) *Anemone* x *hybrida* 'Honorine Jobert' (anemone).

have an interesting winter performance such as that of *Corylus avellana* 'Contorta' with its fascinating skeleton or *Cornus alba* 'Sibirica' with its glowing red stems.

You now have the structure, which you can decorate with the more flamboyant performers from the 'flower' category. These are a mixture of perennials, shrubs and bulbs and should be grouped in clumps of odd numbers to produce drifts of colour. Do not plant in straight lines unless the design specification calls for it. The addition of bulbs will bring an extra dimension to your scheme. Their greatest strength is the small amount of room that they occupy, which enables them to be planted closely around other plants so that their blooms spring from another's foliage. Don't space the bulbs too far apart as their impact depends upon bold sweeps of the same genus.

Having convinced you of the need to mix your borders, I must also explain the argument for the use of single-genus schemes in a contemporary design. Geometric clumps of a flower or shrub in a single colour can provide a striking feature. Most of the plants in the 'feature' category would do well in a scheme such as this; at the other end of the scale, they can excel if given a starring role as a single plant in an urn or container.

Many of the plants in my lists fall into more than one of the three categories of foliage, flower and feature, so I have categorized them according to their main strength.

KNOTS, PARTERRES, POTAGERS AND MAZES

Knots, parterres, potagers and mazes, used in gardens for centuries, are the epitome of formal design, but can be given a more modern twist by experimentation with contemporary shapes and patterns. Usually defined by low evergreen hedging, they can range from the simplest of geometric patterns to the

most intricate. Your imagination is the limit. As if guiding a pencil over paper, you can draw your designs on the earth with lines of planting. But first, 'The beginning of all knowledge starts with the naming of things', so:

A *parterre* is a simple pattern on the ground, in low planting, visible from a window and often the start of a vista.

A *knot* is similar to a parterre, but it can be either open or closed. In an open knot the shapes are individually contained, whereas in a closed knot the lines of planting weave in and out of one another.

A *potager* is a parterre with the spaces that are created filled with vegetables and herbs.

Simplicity is the key to an elegant open knot. If repeating a simple design, incorporating narrow paths and standard trees can help to punctuate the scheme.

A maze has lines of planting that create several pathways to a central point. If the maze has only one route through its design it is a labyrinth.

How do you use these within your own garden? To create shapes and paths that have visible patterns, the minimum area you need is 3x3m (10x10ft). This will not give you enough room for standard paths, but within a parterre design you can get away with paths as narrow as 50cm (20in). Just don't try pushing a barrow down them! If you have only a small area, don't be put off: the essence of a parterre or knot can be achieved by planting small geometric shapes along a pathway or simply an interwoven low hedge along the front of a border. If you are fortunate enough to have a large garden, the ideal place for your parterre is close to the house, where it can be viewed from upstairs windows, and at right angles to the building to be used as part of a vista, or view, up the garden. However, if you are attempting a contemporary design of an abstract shape, the siting is really up to you, although a first-floor view would still be appropriate.

Hedge planting and maintenance

PLANT	DISTANCE	CLIPPING TIME
Santolina chamaecyparissus	20cm (8in) apart	Clip twice: spring and summer
Lavandula angustifolia 'Hidcote'	30cm (1ft) apart	Clip twice: spring and summer
Buxus sempervirens	40cm (15in) apart	Clip twice: spring and summer

As for the materials, gravel is by far the most useful hard landscape surface as it can be spread right up to the stems of plants, giving a simple and uniform colour to set them off. Over-complicated hard landscaping will confuse the eye. Your design, and not the paving, should shine. There are several plants that are suitable for low hedges. The most common is

This superb example of an intricate closed knot is enough to put anyone off clipping forever. Knot gardens are only for the truly dedicated gardener, and those with enough space to do the pattern justice.

ordinary box, *Buxus sempervirens*. Although this plant will grow to 2m (6½ft) if left unclipped, it can be kept short and neat, giving a really solid hedge. There is a dwarf form, 'Suffruticosa', which will reach only 30cm (1ft) in four years, so it requires less clipping, but it will take longer to form a dense hedge and can be a bit hard to find. Second favourite has to be lavender. Use a good-growing ordinary variety like 'Hidcote' with its deep purple blooms. Add cotton lavender (*Santolina chamaecyparissus*), which has silver foliage and lemon flowers, and you have a fantastic three-colour mix for a closed knot. The table on page 86 shows optimum planting distances and clipping times for the three plants described.

Lavandula angustifolia 'Hidcote' (Lavender).

The spaces within knots were often planted, usually with bold and vivid annuals. I make no secret of my dislike for swathes of gaudy annuals, which I call 'municipal parks planting', but it can be done with style, especially if you stick to one genus and colour. It would even be possible to create a transient knot using annuals as the main plants, although the essence of a knot is that it looks as good in the middle of winter, dusted with frost, as it does on a warm summer day.

PLANTS FOR THEMED GARDENS

As ideas for your own design develop, you may find yourself falling into one of the style categories. This does not mean that you need to be a slave to the theme you have chosen. A balance needs to be struck between capturing the essence of the style you desire and the practicalities of using the relevant plants in your particular garden. A small area of an overall scheme may

be given over to a theme: for example, a formal box garden directly in front of a house can give way to a surrounding area of woodland, or the combination of two styles such as minimalism and Mediterranean can offer endless opportunities to develop your own unique space.

Tumbling riotous planting — the epitome of cottage chaos. Allow your plants, especially the annuals, a little freedom to creep on to the paths.

Cottage

To create a cottage garden you need romantic chocolate-box planting: roses, hollyhocks, delphiniums and geraniums packed one on top of the other, flowing out of the beds on to crunchy gravel paths, with spires of sweet peas climbing willow obelisks. The secret to this type of planting is a range of perennials in soft pastel colours with plants massed together.

Woodland

Think of a woodland glade with soft, moist moss underfoot and shafts of sunlight punctuating the leafy canopy. Scatter ferns and spires of *Digitalis purpurea* f. *albiflora* in random clumps. Informal paths wind between sweet-scented *Convallaria*, and hostas' subtle mauve flowers stand erect over abundant foliage.

A spirit level is essential for clipping your hedges in a formal scheme. All the borders are in perfect line and perfect symmetry – not a style for the scruffy gardener.

Formal

Whether in contemporary or historical style, formal planting is evergreen, clipped and regimented: hedges of box (*Buxus sempervirens*) in symmetrical patterns with centrepieces of topiary or taller swathes of yew (*Taxus baccata*) clipped to house alcoves of statuary. Pyramids of bay (*Laurus nobilis*) may punctuate pathways. This style is only for the very neat gardener.

Contemporary

A contemporary garden relies heavily on hard landscaping. The amount of planting may be small, but this makes it all the more important to use good single sculptural specimens. Try bamboos with their stems of lime green or black; and concrete planters softened by rows of blue *Carex* grasses. For a slightly more feminine feature, cover a wall with *Jasminum officinale*, which has delicate green leaves and pure white star flowers.

(Opposite) If only we all had enough room to grow a copse of trees. Instead, take inspiration from the informal scheme and use of height.

Oriental

Simple and restrained planting is the trademark of an oriental garden. The use of the colour green predominates in all its shades and leaf forms. Bushes such as *Buxus sempervirens* and azalea clipped into soft mounds depicting miniature mountain ranges; a lush green carpet of *Soleirolia soleirolii* punctuated by stepping stones; and a single specimen tree – perhaps a pine or *Acer palmatum* – often contorted into a weather-ravaged form, represent the epitome of oriental style. Think calm, spiritual, understated simplicity.

Mediterranean

Bold and shocking colours that come alive with a sprinkling of sunshine bring Mediterranean style to the garden. Choose tender plants such as cascades of gaudy red pelargoniums and billowing pink bougainvillea; and specimen citrus trees in terra-cotta pots, mixed with spiky drought-lovers like phormiums and cordylines that cast intriguing shadows on to azure-coloured walls. These plants are not for the faint-hearted.

PREPARING TO PLANT

Most gardening books will tell you it is essential to identify the type of soil that you have in your plot before designing the garden. I would agree to a certain extent, but the choice of plants for new gardeners is already bewildering and the thought of having to assess each specimen's pH level is enough to send them into a blind panic. Don't worry: the process of identifying soil pH need not be as intimidating as you might think. There are plenty of soil-testing kits on the market and they do a pretty good job. However, if you just observe the kind of plants that your neighbours are growing, you can tell what the soil is

The adventurous gardener may try a Mediterranean scheme, but only if you have the courage to go for it. Colours must be vibrant, pigment-based shades in blue, orange and yellow.

(Above) A minimal garden that uses shadows cast by branches as a sculptural feature against a stark sandy-coloured wall. Don't overclutter your scheme, to obtain this look you need to hold back.

(Far right) A modern scheme can rely on only one or two genera. But, as in this garden, they must be large, specimen-sized plants in order to counterbalance the hard landscaping.

(Right) Apparently, raking your gravel helps to calm your soul. This garden relies on the patterns made on the ground to link the standing stones into a scheme. Remember to work backwards or you'll see your footprints.

like in your area. If they are all growing azaleas, ericas and rhododendrons, you can assume that the soil is quite acidic, but what you need to know about most plants is that they will quite happily tolerate soil that is neutral, slightly acidic or slightly alkaline.

It is always possible to change the pH level of an acidic garden using lime, but this will work for only one season and you will have begun a life-long fight with your flowerbeds to alter what nature has given you. Far better to go with the flow.

Digitalis purpurea (foxglove).

If you have acidic soil, learn to love acid-loving plants – unless the level is particularly acidic, you will find you can grow a lot of other plants too.

Soils are classified by the proportion of sand, clay and loam they contain. To find out what yours is, you need to assess its texture. This is the best bit. Go outside with a bucket of water and make some mud pies. No, I haven't gone mad – and wearing a pair of gloves is not on. You will need to feel the texture of the soil in your hand.

Dampen the soil with a little water and assess its contents:

- *Is it slimy and full of clay?*
- *Does it clump into one large ball?*
- *Does it crumble and refuse to hold a shape even when squeezed?*

You will find it useful to follow the flow chart on page 95.

There are advantages and disadvantages whatever type of soil you have. Sandy soil is easier to dig, but this means that it is also free-draining, so it loses nutrients as rainwater permeates it. It will need regular irrigation and feeding. However, the

How to identify your soil type

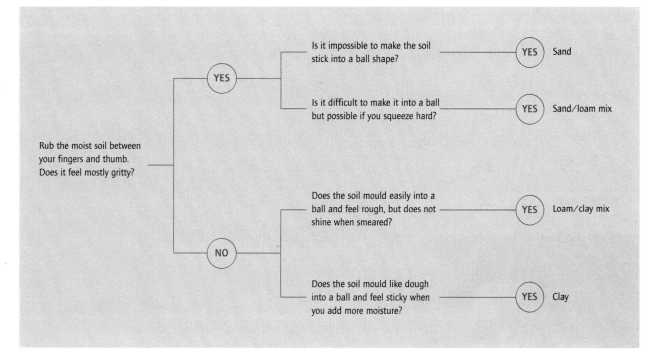

upside is that it warms up quickly in spring. While clay soil is rich and full of nutrients, it is also prone to large areas of puddling where the ground is compacted and water cannot easily permeate and, in times of drought, will bake to a crust that is almost impossible to dig.

What we are aiming for is a soil with good drainage and plenty of organic matter, one that is friable and pleasing to the touch. There are several ways to achieve this. If you have very difficult clay soil that is undiggable in winter and a concrete crust in summer, the only solution may be to remove the top 30cm (1ft) and replace it with good topsoil – a radical solution for a worst-case scenario only. To loosen up slightly clay soil, spread a layer of horticultural grit or fine gravel about 5cm (2 in) thick on your border and fork it in. This will make the soil more free-draining and easier to work. Then add gardener's gold – well-rotted organic matter. You will also need to add plenty of this to sandy soil to provide nutrients and help make the soil more cohesive.

Organic matter is available in many forms, the least expensive of which being animal manure. In my experience it doesn't matter if it's horse or cow – in fact I have even tried elephant, which has the added advantage of arriving in very large quantities – but whichever you choose, it must be extremely well rotted. Dig from the bottom of the pile. If the manure is slimy or smells awful, don't use it. Well-rotted manure should crumble and smell good enough to touch.

Clematis armandii 'Apple Blossom'.

If raw poo is too much for you, there are plenty of commercial soil improvers on the market, available from garden centres in nice clean bags, although you may find yourself paying quite a lot for the convenience.

The third option, if you can find it, is spent mushroom compost. Made from a mixture of manure and straw, this is pasteurized and originally used to grow mushrooms commercially. After so many weeks it is disposed of and, if you are lucky, available to buy for your garden. This material is the best soil conditioner. You know it will do the garden good just by the appearance of it – crumbly and dark, it smells like warm cat's paws.

Last, and the most satisfactory source of organic matter, is home-made compost. Turning the organic waste from your house into a soil improver is eco-friendly and very satisfying. To make it, two compost bins are best, one 'cooking' and one filling. Everyone has their own recipe for making a successful heap. I never turn mine, but I do add a little manure every 60cm (2ft) and my husband pees in a watering can, whose contents I water down and pour on the heap. I would do this myself, only women's plumbing and watering cans – need I say more?

Alchemilla mollis (lady's mantle).

NATURE VERSUS NURTURE

Plants are the living, breathing soul of your garden. Even with the best-laid plans you are not likely to get your planting schemes completely right first time. This does not necessarily mean that you got it wrong. Instead of feeling like a failure, consider each setback as a piece of knowledge acquired about your own garden. When a plant fails, try it again. If it fails twice, perhaps it is not right for that particular spot.

Galanthus (snowdrop).

When a plant is so successful that it invades every nook of a border, be ruthless and keep it in check. You must be in charge of your border and not the other way round. Even in a crowded cottage-garden scheme you need to organize your chaos.

Be aware of shrubs that are getting too large for their situation and try to prune them before they are too big. Rescue attempts are no substitute for good maintenance. Don't be afraid of pruning: it is extremely hard to kill a plant in this way. The worst damage you will do is reduce its flowering capacity for the following season.

As for perennials, be generous. When they have been established for three to four years, dig them up and split them into smaller clumps, putting back some new healthy growth and giving the spare plants to friends. With luck they will give you some of their border overflow in return. In my own garden there is many a plant known only by the name of the person who shared it with me.

The fourth dimension in your garden is time. Don't try to fight it. Allow the borders to grow, spread and evolve. Do keep hold of your initial scheme, but perhaps allow Mother Nature to intervene now and then.

(Opposite) *Eremurus* (Foxtail lily).

GETTING STARTED
THE PRACTICALITIES

I hope that by this stage in the book you are full of ideas and enthusiasm and are raring to go. However, there are some more mundane matters that need addressing before you can implement your great plans. The time has come to become acquainted with surveying.

Surveying sounds scarier than it really is, but it is important that you can take basic ground measurements and translate them into a scale plan. All you need for laying out your ideas is a very simple drawing of your garden.

You might be tempted just to look out of the window and draw a freehand sketch of the shape and proportion that you think the garden has. Don't do it. Your eye is not accurate enough. For instance, you could well be surprised to discover that what you think is a square is in fact a parallelogram (most are). Features that you will want to include in your design are the minimum widths, heights and proportions of objects. They will need lining up with existing points of the garden and house and, if the plan you use is not reasonably accurate, your garden design will not fit or, worse still, will jar and look very obviously amateurish.

SURVEYING A REGULAR PLOT

If you have a simple four-sided plot you need only six measurements (illustrated overleaf on Diagram 1). The two diagonal measurements are most important as very few plots

You will need:
- Pencil
- Eraser
- Plain paper
- Rough paper
- Tape measure – the longer the better
- Compass
- Scale ruler
- Patience

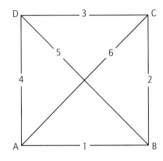

Diagram 1

are indeed square. If you do not have a tape measure long enough for these measurements, lay a piece of rope or hosepipe on the ground and measure in sections along it. Having taken your measurements and worked out the scale you are going to use – I usually use 1cm:1m (1in:6ft) – begin by drawing line AB to scale on your paper.

Then, to find the position of point C (see Diagram 2): with the compass set at length AC and the compass point in A, draw an arc. With the compass set at length BC and the point in B, draw another arc. Where the two arcs cross is point C.

To find the position of point D (see Diagram 3): with the compass set at length AD and the point in A, draw an arc. With the compass set at length BD and the point in B, draw another arc. Where the two arcs cross is point D. Now draw in lines BC and AD and join point C to point D to complete the basic site plan.

Check your plan by measuring line CD on the scale drawing and comparing it to the measurement you took on the ground. Don't be too hard on yourself if it is a little out. Now mark the position of your house in relation to the garden.

Diagram 2

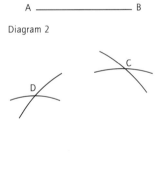

Diagram 3

Once you have your basic site plan, there are two things you must never forget to mark on it: the scale of the drawing and its orientation (that is, which direction is north). If you don't have a walkers' compass, just remember that the sun rises in the east and sets in the west. Then, when you have completed your site plan to your satisfaction, take several photocopies of your original drawing, so that you can keep making revisions.

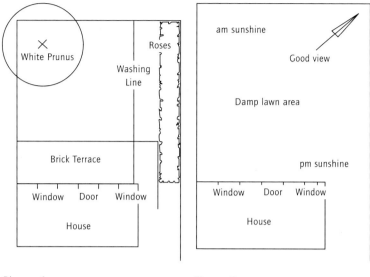

Diagram 4   Diagram 5

On the first site plan copy, mark on any features of the garden that you wish to keep. Do this for both hard and soft landscaping. Once again, try to keep the features to scale. This will help with redesigning. When it comes to trees, put an X where the trunk is and then a circle for the area that its canopy covers (approximately will do). Don't forget to include the washing line, existing paving, sheds, etc., and any doors that open on to the garden (see Diagram 4).

On another site plan copy, take time to observe your garden and mark on how the elements affect your space. Is there a particularly sunny spot? Are there two – one in the morning and one in the evening? Is the garden always in total shade? Does a tree or feature interrupt your view? Is there a particularly draughty area where the wind howls through? Does one area of the lawn always flood? Mark also the views that you have from your property, particularly the ones you appreciate regularly – for example, from the kitchen window (see Diagram 5).

Lastly, if you can, mark where the drains run across the garden, or any power cables, over- or underground. If, like me, you are reliant on a septic tank, mark that on the plan too, including the soakaway.

SURVEYING AN IRREGULAR PLOT

Not many people have a square plot, but this simple square surveying technique is the basis for all shapes of garden. First, try to find a basic square within your plot (marked A/B/C/D on Diagram 6). Mark it out, putting a stake at each corner. Measure the basic square and transfer the measurements to your scale plan. Mark points at set intervals along the sides of the basic square. Now measure from these points to the boundary of your garden. Transfer these measurements to your scale plan and join the ends of these points, rather like dot-to-dot. (Now add the house and then proceed from Diagram 4 for regular plots.)

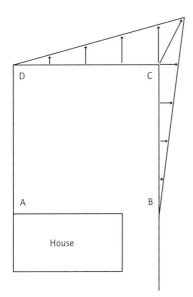

Diagram 6

SURVEYING THE LEVEL

The other important factor when surveying your plot is its level. If your garden has a drop in level already absorbed into steps or a terrace (see Diagram 7), mark this on the site plan. It will be easy to measure your overall drop (BC) by measuring each step and the distance it travels (AB).

If, however, there is just a slope (see Diagram 8), attach a piece of string at the highest point A, hold it horizontally and let the rest of the string fall vertically from B. You can judge the horizontal by eye, but it is better to rely on a spirit level. You can now measure your overall drop (BC), and the distance it travels (AB).

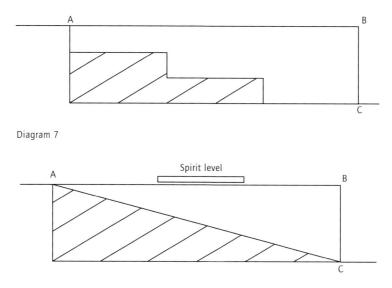

Diagram 7

Diagram 8

DESIGNING ON PLAN

So you've read the book. You know what you want in your garden. You've thought about materials and features to include. Now, armed with your two annotated site plans as reference, and your lists of 'Have', 'Want' and 'Need' (see page 16), along with your inspirational pictures and photographs, the time has come to stop reading and start designing. It does not matter what level your drawing skills are, for sticks and blobs will do just fine.

On the blank, photocopied site plans, mark any existing features you wish to keep and then start roughly marking on where the *new* features will go. At this stage it is best to draw them in free-hand. Don't get bogged down with a scale rule or a compass. Just scribble, trying to establish two good variations on your theme (see Diagrams 9 and 10 overleaf), and keep referring back to your notes. You might find it hard to get started but, once you have gained a little confidence, you will

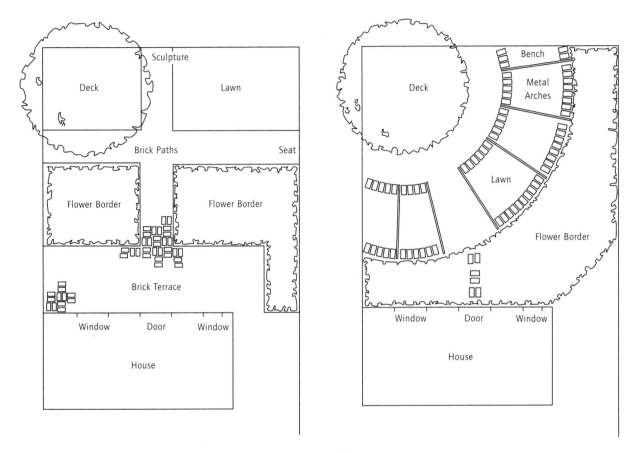

Diagram 9

Diagram 10

find the permutations are endless and it is difficult to know when to stop.

When you have exhausted your design variations, settle on the plan you like best and begin to refine the design. You may find that you like most of one plan with a feature from another, so a combination of two plans will be needed. Don't try to combine too many plans together or the garden will look uncoordinated and overcrowded. Keep the design as simple as possible.

Begin refining your drawing using a scale rule to make paths and features the right size; use a compass for any curves or circles and begin to put in notes on the landscape materials you have chosen. Refer back to the site plan showing doors and windows to make sure that paths are in the right place and views of the garden are pleasing from each window. You might find it useful to add some colour at this stage. It need only be pencil crayon for the lawn and borders, but it helps to give a sense of the finished garden.

Be bold with your shapes; try to echo one shape several times. Drawing concentric circles or squares can offer great possibilities, or try a motif like an oblong and tessellate with it, always keeping in mind Fibonacci's theory (see pages 12–14) and dividing the space into thirds. Spirals are another pleasing shape, as are interlocking curves, for a gentle informal garden. Draw the shapes first and then decide which bit of shape will become lawn or patio. Draw over your existing garden features, even if they are to stay. An existing patio does not have to remain the same shape; it can be expanded to fit the new scheme.

One other golden rule: never try to design one corner of your garden while ignoring the rest of the plot. If you want your design to have a rhythmic and harmonious style, you must address the garden as one design project. This does not mean that the garden must be built in one go. If there are financial considerations, design the garden as a whole and then build in stages.

When you feel you are getting attractive shapes and features in the right place, a good trick to get an idea of the look of the finished garden is to take photographs of your plot as it is at present. Do this from key vantage points, such as doors or paths. Next place a piece of drawing film (tracing paper will do) over the photograph and sketch on the new features. This will give you a rough idea as to whether you have got the look of the garden right.

MARKING OUT

Don't put a spade in the ground until you have marked out your garden design. This is your last chance to see if you have made some crushingly bad errors in your plan. You are effectively redrawing your scale plan on the ground using a spray can, rope or sand, which gives you the opportunity to walk along the paths, look back down the vistas and sit on the imaginary patio. Does your garden design work?

By far the easiest material to use for marking out is a paint spray can. You can get special designing mark-out paint from builders' merchants or use a left-over can of car paint from the shed. If you prefer, a trail of sand will do the trick, although it is all too easy to scuff it out. Failing that, a rope along the ground kept taut by stakes will do, but don't go roaming around the garden at night.

First, a word of warning: if someone is helping you to measure out the plot, make sure that you are both using the same system of measurement (metric or imperial, not a mixture). It sounds obvious, but mistakes have been made.

Straight lines are a doddle to mark out. Mark either end and join up the point. Do use a plank as a straight edge – your eye will not do, unless you want crooked paths.

Diagram 11

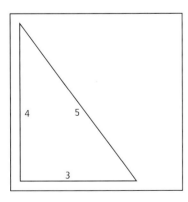

If you want to create a right angle when you are marking out, use a simple 3–4–5 triangle (see Diagram 11). Using a surveyor's tape you can mark out a triangle with sides measuring 3, 4 and 5m long. This will always give you a perfect right angle. If these measurements are too long for the space you have available, you can use a triangle of 3, 4 and 5 feet, or even centimetres: it is the ratio between the numbers that is important.

Circles are relatively simple to mark out. Mark the centre of your circle on the ground by taking two measurements from points on the design that already exist, such as a corner of the house or windows. Where the measurements from these static points cross is the middle of your circle (see Diagram 12). Put a cane in this point and, using a piece of rope marked at the correct radius of your circle, draw a line, keeping the string taut at all times.

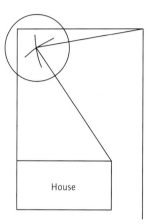

House

Diagram 12

Curves or semi-circles must always be marked out in the same way as circles. If you try to do them by eye, they will always be slightly 'off' and lack the professional touch.

Ovals are a little more tricky but worth the effort. By placing two stakes in the ground and tying a length of string in a large loop around them, as long as you keep the string taut and in contact with both stakes you will be able to draw a perfect oval (see Diagram 13).

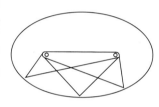

Diagram 13

If you are siting a pergola or archway use 2m (6½ft) canes pushed into the ground in the required place to give you an idea of its vertical dimensions.

When all this is completed, take a stroll around the marked-out garden. Ask yourself these questions:

- *Are the paths wide enough?*
- *Can I fit a table and chairs on the terrace/deck?*
- *Are the flowerbeds large enough and in proportion with the rest of the design?*
- *Do the vistas line up with windows, doors and features?*
- *Are the features I kept from the original garden sympathetically incorporated into the new design?*

Bearing in mind this may be your first attempt at surveying and setting out a garden, don't be dismayed if your measurements are slightly inaccurate – it happens to the best of us.

When you lay out the design, start with paths and features that line up with windows or doors. If these vistas are wrong, the design will shout 'amateur' at you, so better to get these spot on and fudge the boundary features. A border or lawn that is 30, 60 or even 90cm (1, 2 or 3 ft) out is neither here nor there – unless your scheme is a minimalist one (see page 116).

DEALING WITH DIFFICULT SITES

Not all gardens are created equal. Eden may have been the only perfect site with superb soil and an even climate; most people battle against some fault that nature has dumped in their lap. Wherever possible you must garden in sympathy with your surroundings. There is little point in trying to create a tender tropical paradise if your garden is susceptible to east winds and the temperature regularly drops below freezing. You can spend more time wrapping your plants in fleece than enjoying the garden's ambience. So let us tackle some of the most common problems and the best ways to deal with them.

Wind

Under no circumstances put up a solid fence to try to stop the gusts – it will blow down. Plant hedging along your boundary and consider dividing the garden into smaller sections, using more hedge to interrupt the flow. If space allows, a small grove of trees within your garden will also help. Find the spot where there is most shelter and develop this as your sitting area, with the addition of a pergola or summer house, for further shelter.

Soil

It is important to determine whether you have sandy or clay soil, so follow the flow diagram on page 95 to work out your soil type.

North-Facing, Heavy Shade

These conditions are not ideal if you are a sun-seeker, but very few gardens have complete shade. Observe where your pockets of light fall and use these areas for terrace and benches. As for the deep shade, don't battle with plants that want sun, but revel in the marvellous foliage choices that crave these sheltered situations. Concentrate on foliage, shades of green and white flowers. Shy away from blues as they can look dull in shade and, if you must have colour, try incorporating glazed pots and painted walls. An oriental garden can thrive in a shady situation but, whatever hard landscaping you use, keep a watch on algae, which can grow at an alarming rate, making surfaces treacherous to walk on.

South-Facing, Too Much Sun

Your first priority is to give the garden some height and structure to create shade. Pergolas and arches provide instant shelter with the addition of some fast-growing climbers. In a garden that is baked by sun, getting enough water to your borders will always be a problem. An integral irrigation system will help, along with thick mulch, geotextile membrane and dense planting. Look for plants that will stand full-sun conditions; if you are lucky enough to have a sheltered spot as well as a south aspect, a Mediterranean garden will thrive.

Long, Thin Site

'How do I make my long thin garden look shorter?' is a question I regularly have to tackle. 'Why would you want to?' is usually my response. As far as I am concerned, the more odd the shape of your plot, the better but, for advice on dealing with a long thin site, see page 152.

A long site gives you the opportunity for vistas, elegant views down sinuous paths. Use walls or trellis to divide the space so that there are obstacles to traverse to find the end of your garden. Mirrors are a great way to fool the viewer. Set into doorways in boundary walls, they give the impression of a further garden to explore.

Wide, Short Site

If you are fortunate enough to have a view at the end of your short plot, don't put up a solid barrier. Steal the landscape from outside your garden. You can still define the boundary with a fence, but make it low and permeable.

On the other hand you may need to erect a standard 2m (6 ½ft) boundary and this will give the garden a feeling of claustrophobia, so make the boundary as subtle as possible. You don't want it to shout out: 'Here is the end of the garden.' Use a material that blends with your scheme and then place other design items in front so that the viewer never has a clear look at the boundary. Finally, the easiest trick is to divert the eye away on a diagonal axis towards the corner of the garden, giving the impression of a longer plot.

Noise Pollution

Very few of us live in an area where we are not subjected to some kind of noise pollution, be it caused by voices, road traffic, aeroplanes or industry. They can all spoil the oasis of calm that a garden should be. It is not possible to eliminate all of the unwanted sound, but you can certainly soften it. If you imagine a room without furniture or carpet, it is noisy and the sound bounces around. Once the soft furnishings are in, the atmosphere changes to a muffled quiet. This will also happen in a garden. Here your soft furnishings are represented by the plants and lawn, cushioning you against the ambient noise, and with larger plants, such as trees and bamboos, the gentle rustle of their leaves in the breeze will cover unwanted sounds.

The murmur of running water in your garden can also help, not to drown out the pollution but to distract your ear so that it tunes in to the water feature rather than the surrounding noise. (See pages 58–71 for information on water features.)

Lastly, a mound of earth around the garden with a swathe of trees will deaden traffic noise, although most of us don't have a plot big enough to warrant earthworks on this scale.

Ugly View

For ways to distract attention from an ugly view, see page 51.

Sloping Site

Try to think of your slope as a gift rather than a problem. Admittedly there are slopes and there are slopes. If your garden closely resembles Val-d'Isère, you have a problem. The plot will need to be split into terraces, cutting huge steps into your slope. This is not a problem for a good builder or hard landscaper, but I would hesitate to try to tackle it yourself – you could wake up one morning to find the whole garden at the bottom of your slope.

Decking can be a life-saver in these cases. Less expensive than building retaining walls, it can easily create level changes. Try not to cut your garden into terraces from side to side, but use the fall of the land to give you interesting sections of deck at quirky angles. (See 'A Coastal Garden' on page 140 for some ideas.)

If you are coping with a gentle slope, water is an excellent feature to incorporate. Whether formal or informal in style, water cascading down level changes gives instant impact in the garden.

DESIGNS

W hen I set out to write this book, it was always my intention to illustrate my design style with several sample gardens. The chance to design with a free hand, to put each feature within a garden exactly where I wanted and to use any material I chose was an exciting prospect – I was power-crazed and full of extravagant ideas. It was only moments later that it occurred to me that the task ahead, which had at first seemed like a heavenly prospect, as I would be designing without clients' restraints, was in fact hell – no, worse, it was impossible. I realized that, even when I design show gardens where I am free to let my imagination run wild, I am always conscious of the people who would live with my designs, as well as subliminally aware of their needs and wants, how they would use their outdoor space and their attitude to gardening.

So, I decided that each of the following eight designs would need a household of imaginary people, covering all levels of gardening interest, different tastes and style as well as geographical position. You might think that I chose the easy way out by creating designs for nice, neat, identically-sized plots, but I want to try to show you how differently you can use the same garden space. I am not suggesting that you will necessarily find yourself among these households but, by studying the design choices I have made for them, you may be able to translate some of these ideas to your own garden.

(Above) Restraint, and the mixture of clean lines of steel with the transparent sheet of glass, give this small space a clean, uncluttered feel.

(Opposite) This award-winning garden by Christopher Bradley-Hole shows all that is good in garden design; from the skilful use of colour, to the powerful vertical accent of the concrete walls.

A STYLISH MINIMAL GARDEN

Who They Are
HOME
Basement flat with two bedrooms, all on one floor, in urban location. The sitting room and kitchen look out on to the garden.

OCCUPATION
Couple, both working professionals (full-time). Young and enthusiastic.

CHILDREN
One toddler boy.

STYLE:
Ultra-modern. Minimalist. Conran; Paul Smith, Muji. Clean lines, uncluttered spaces.

TIME
Although they are enthusiastic about a new garden, they have only about four hours a week between them to garden.

Entering the garden from the house leads you down a path between four symmetrical square raised beds, each one planted with a lawn and constructed in cast polished concrete. This material is a refined version of its common cousin, with a soft white sheen and smooth satin finish. The path takes you to a water feature flush with the ground. A bridge of cast concrete travels on to a central square, over the water rill and across a second bridge. The water flows from the central pond down the two rills and into the large ponds. As the owners have a small child, the deep water is protected by a grid of wavy stainless-steel rods set into the concrete at water level. Should anyone fall into the pond, this grid will be strong enough to hold them. At night the water is illuminated with a gentle glow from underwater spotlights.

The last area has four symmetrical square borders, each containing two genera of plants: a bulb for spring or autumn flower and a perennial for summer. All the flowers are white and are set off against the deep green background of the hedge of pleached limes that encloses the back of the garden. The hedge grows from a trench covered in white 'dinosaur egg' cobbles.

Turning right at the top of the garden leads you on to the raised play lawn, large enough to picnic or sunbathe on, with a view of the borders. The lawn also looks on to four more beds with a tall square pillar of box (*Buxus sempervirens*) at the centre of each square and a carpet of mind-your-own-business at its feet.

The garden culminates in a cast-concrete seating area of two L-shaped benches with a strip of glass blocks at floor level as underfloor lighting. The pleached limes are lit by thousands of white fairy lights entwined in the branches. The plants, lights and features are all reflected in eight square mirrors set on the boundary walls, which are rendered smooth and painted pale grey.

What They Have
Dingy, dark, north-facing, brick-walled yard. One access point to the yard through the sitting room and house. Overlooked on every side by neighbouring properties.

What They Want
Chic, uncluttered, startling and modern space, to entertain, relax and make love in.

What They Need
Space to let light into the flat. Somewhere safe and stimulating for the child to play and somewhere to hang washing.

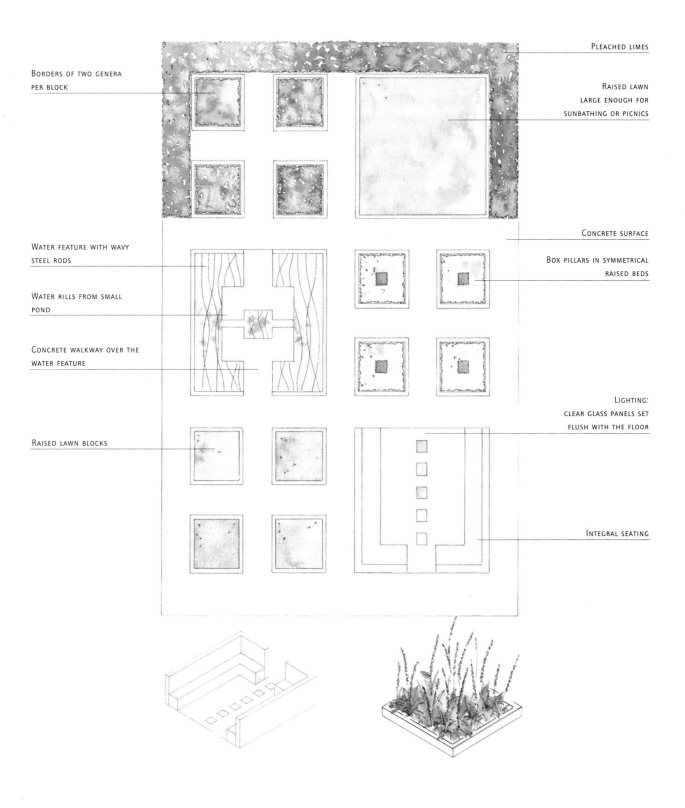

PLEACHED LIMES

BORDERS OF TWO GENERA
PER BLOCK

RAISED LAWN
LARGE ENOUGH FOR
SUNBATHING OR PICNICS

WATER FEATURE WITH WAVY
STEEL RODS

CONCRETE SURFACE

BOX PILLARS IN SYMMETRICAL
RAISED BEDS

WATER RILLS FROM SMALL
POND

CONCRETE WALKWAY OVER THE
WATER FEATURE

LIGHTING:
CLEAR GLASS PANELS SET
FLUSH WITH THE FLOOR

RAISED LAWN BLOCKS

INTEGRAL SEATING

Planting List

SQUARE BORDERS
Cimicifuga racemosa
(bugbane)
Colchicum speciosum
'Album'
(autumn crocus)
Crocus sieberi 'Bowles'
White'
Digitalis purpurea f.
albiflora (foxglove)
Galanthus nivalis
(snowdrop)
Leucojum vernum
(snowflake)
Polygonatum biflorum
(Solomon's seal)
Veronica longifolia 'Alba'
(speedwell)

COLUMN BORDER
Buxus sempervirens (box)
Soleirolia soleirolii (mind-
your-own-business)

PLEACHED HEDGE
Tilia oliveri (lime)

TRANSLATION TO OTHER DESIGNS

Pleached trees are one of my favourite design tools. Their use is neglected, usually because they take anything from two to five years to form a solid structure, but they are worth the time and effort. Use them to line an avenue or, as I have here, place them to surround the end of a design as a sort of horticultural full stop. They work equally well in soft sculptural lines as they do in straight formal schemes. Try planting them in a circle, but only three-quarters of the way round, leaving one-quarter unplanted, and you have a spectacular foil for a central sculpture; or make a small U-shape to enclose a lovers' seat.

Raising the beds and lawn gives a garden instant interest. It only has to be one step up to have the desired effect and it would work equally well with a retaining wall made from railway sleepers or blue brick. You could also try dropping the level of a feature down by one step, although you need to be aware of waterlogging. If you are in an area prone to this type of problem, combine an area of one step up with an area of one step down and the effect is to draw the viewer into the garden space: a useful trick if you are trying to take the eye away from a boundary eyesore.

Using the same proportions and measurements throughout a design is vital in a reserved and formal scheme like this. The mirrors are exactly the same size as the square raised beds; the path across the water feature is the same width as the path between the raised beds; the sunken lights are the same dimensions as the box pillars. This might not seem important, but it is attention to the details of measurement that adds a professional touch. In minimal schemes there is nowhere to hide – get the dimensions wrong and you might as well forget the whole design.

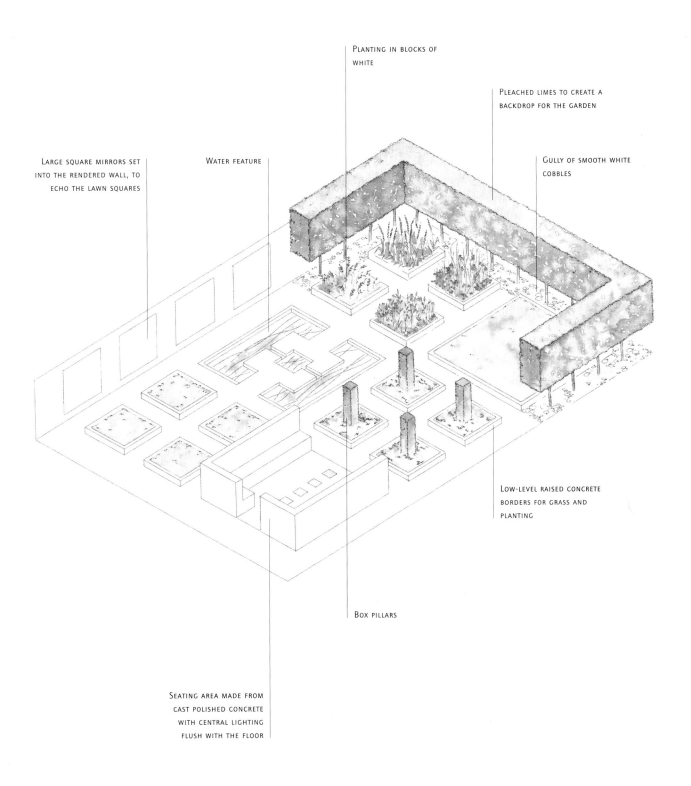

PLANTING IN BLOCKS OF
WHITE

PLEACHED LIMES TO CREATE A
BACKDROP FOR THE GARDEN

LARGE SQUARE MIRRORS SET
INTO THE RENDERED WALL, TO
ECHO THE LAWN SQUARES

WATER FEATURE

GULLY OF SMOOTH WHITE
COBBLES

LOW-LEVEL RAISED CONCRETE
BORDERS FOR GRASS AND
PLANTING

BOX PILLARS

SEATING AREA MADE FROM
CAST POLISHED CONCRETE
WITH CENTRAL LIGHTING
FLUSH WITH THE FLOOR

A SUBURBAN FAMILY GARDEN

Who They Are

HOME
Three-bedroom estate property with access via a path down side of house.

OCCUPATION
He works full-time, she is a full-time mother.

CHILDREN
Two boys aged three and seven; one girl aged eleven.

STYLE
They like things pretty and soft – nothing too modern or stark.

TIME
He will mow the lawn, but that is all. She is keen to learn, but has limited knowledge of gardening and a busy schedule. They have about four hours per week between them to garden.

The main access to the garden leads you through double doors on to a narrow slab path that creates a central vista underneath five metal arches dripping with clematis. To the right is an area for outside dining with plenty of room for a barbecue and table and chairs, and to the left is a mirror-image space to be used as a lounge with comfortable steamer chairs. The surface of these areas is inexpensive concrete slabs, laid chequer-board style with turf, and each side has three planting pits to enable climbers to scramble over the painted fence.

The central feature of the garden is a circular lawn surrounded by a flower border filled with a good range of shrubs, perennials and bulbs in blues, pinks and purples. Around this border is a circular path of concrete slabs mixed with waste slate laid on end, and beyond that a further lawn encloses the whole scheme. The very centre of this area has a small cast circle of concrete with the hand prints of all the children and a hole for the rotary washing line. Two slab paths lead off the circular path through a tall semi-circular hedge of native plants such as hawthorn, holly, blackthorn and elder. These are inexpensive plants that will knit into a loose hedge of foliage, berry and blossom and fill with wildlife. A second hedge gives a corridor for the children to race around and a

What They Have

A rectangle of grass, with two existing trees and orange-stained larch-lap fencing, plus neighbours looking in on all sides, on a modern estate. With three children of between three and eleven, their budget for the garden is tight.

What They Want

He will garden reluctantly, and so far has only ever grown Busy Lizzie (*Impatiens*) in pots. Busy with the children, she wants low-maintenance, but aspires to be a gardener. Both would like a barbecue and an area for eating outside. The children want excitement, space and a lawn with somewhere for adventure play.

What They Need

Space for the three children to play. Low to medium maintenance or their initial interest in gardening will dwindle. A terrace for entertaining, eating outside and sunbathing.

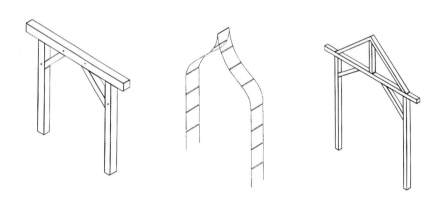

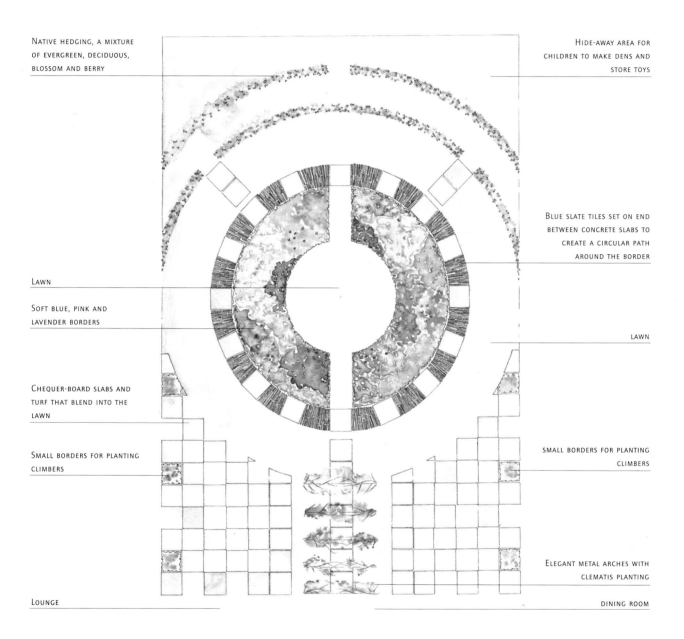

NATIVE HEDGING, A MIXTURE
OF EVERGREEN, DECIDUOUS,
BLOSSOM AND BERRY

HIDE-AWAY AREA FOR
CHILDREN TO MAKE DENS AND
STORE TOYS

BLUE SLATE TILES SET ON END
BETWEEN CONCRETE SLABS TO
CREATE A CIRCULAR PATH
AROUND THE BORDER

LAWN

SOFT BLUE, PINK AND
LAVENDER BORDERS

LAWN

CHEQUER-BOARD SLABS AND
TURF THAT BLEND INTO THE
LAWN

SMALL BORDERS FOR PLANTING
CLIMBERS

SMALL BORDERS FOR PLANTING
CLIMBERS

ELEGANT METAL ARCHES WITH
CLEMATIS PLANTING

LOUNGE

DINING ROOM

Planting List

CLIMBERS FOR ARCHWAYS
Clematis armandii
(evergreen clematis)
Clematis florida 'Sieboldii'
Clematis 'Henryi'
Clematis 'H. F. Young'

CIRCULAR BORDER
Buddleja davidii 'Peace'
(butterfly bush)
Campanula persicifolia
(bellflower)
Choisya ternata (Mexican
orange blossom)
Corylus avellana
'Contorta' (corkscrew
hazel)
Echinops ritro 'Veitch's
Blue' (globe thistle)
Eremurus robustus (foxtail
lily)
Geranium sanguineum
'Album' (white cranesbill)
Muscari armeniacum
(grape hyacinth)
Nepeta x *faassenii* (catmint)
Papaver orientale
'Mrs Perry' (oriental poppy)
Penstemon 'Apple Blossom'
Philadelphus 'Virginal'
(mock orange)
Phlox paniculata
'White Admiral'
Salvia × *sylvestris*
'Mainacht'
Scilla siberica
Syringa 'Président Grévy'
(lilac)
Tulipa 'Queen of the
Night'
Veronica longifolia
(speedwell)
Weigela florida

second doorway leads to a secret area with bark chippings on the ground, where they can have a den and even a climbing frame or other outdoor toys.

This garden, constructed of inexpensive materials that are readily available and well within the ability of most novice gardeners, shows that you can have a garden for beginners that is full of style and interest.

TRANSLATION TO OTHER DESIGNS

The simple stylish shape of concentric circles in this garden will work easily in a garden of any shape. Put the circle in first and then decide where the paths will go. A cross shape with four paths meeting at a central point will give you space for a bench or urn at the end of each path. Don't always put the border around the edge of a garden. Having access from both sides of a border, as in this design, means ease of maintenance and a spectacular view from both sides.

A chequer-board patio can be achieved with any square paving unit. It is an imaginative way to pep up boring concrete slabs. As long as the turf is laid flush with the slabs you can mow straight over the top of the patio. It will work best in a formal design with straight lines to follow; too many curves and you will have to cut every slab.

HEDGE
Crataegus monogyna
(hawthorn)
Ilex aquifolium (holly)
Prunus spinosa
(blackthorn)
Sambucus nigra (elder)

FENCE BY LOUNGE
Hedera helix (ivy)
Rosa 'Madame Alfred
Carrière' (rose)
Wisteria sinensis

FENCE BY DINING ROOM
Passiflora caerulea
(passion flower)
Solanum crispum
(potato tree)

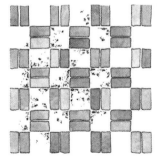
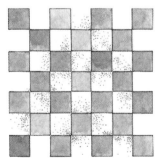

ABUNDANT CLIMBERS OVER
THE BOUNDARY FENCE

NATIVE HEDGE TO DISGUISE
AREA FOR CHILDREN TO PLAY

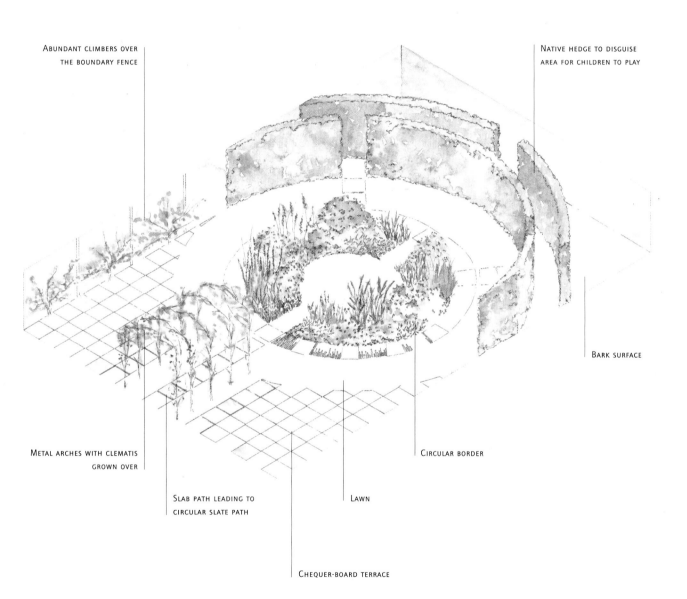

BARK SURFACE

METAL ARCHES WITH CLEMATIS
GROWN OVER

CIRCULAR BORDER

SLAB PATH LEADING TO
CIRCULAR SLATE PATH

LAWN

CHEQUER-BOARD TERRACE

A CITY ROOF GARDEN

Who She Is

HOME
Top-floor flat in city
location with large roof
space, reinforced and
suitable for development
as a garden.

OCCUPATION
Single woman working
full-time with trips out of
the country at least once a
month.

CHILDREN
None.

STYLE
Bold and bright, and
individual in every way.
Very outgoing, loves to
travel and collects items
from journeys. Wouldn't be
caught dead in beige;
loves markets and antique
clothes.

TIME
Very limited time available
to garden – weekends
when not away working,
occasional evenings.
Average only one hour a
week.

As you enter the garden through a hatch, up steep wooden steps from the flat, it hits you with a profusion of bold brash colours: shocking pinks, deep burgundy reds and shades of lavender and navy.

At the north side of the roof is an integral seating unit of lavender-stained wood. Low to the ground and deep, the look is reminiscent of a Bedouin tent with enormous scatter cushions of rich jewel colours. To the back of the seating is a low rendered wall in blue, for safety and to add more colour. From the wall protrude steel poles, also in blue, which taper off near their tip and provide support for several glass panels around two and a half sides of the garden. These allow in light while their frosted pattern gives privacy and the added advantage of shelter from the wind.

The table in the middle of the seating area is a cast-concrete slab with a central planting section, all echoing the elliptical shape of the low-level seat and in a shade of blue to complement the walls.

To the south-east corner of the roof is a large raised bed, constructed of cast concrete and painted blue. This bed is overflowing with low-maintenance planting of mostly evergreen bushes with the occasional shocking bloom: maximum impact for minimum effort. The bed also includes an integral watering system to give the plants much-needed moisture as they are containerized and subject to drying winds.

The permanent dining table, of frosted glass, is suspended by taut steel wires from a guide wire running between two of the blue poles. It is anchored to the roof floor by four more taut wires. For stability the surface under the table is non-slip metal plating decorated with a leaf motif and it is surrounded by lavender-stained decking boards. The entire dining area is

What She Has
Roof space with hatch
access, overlooked by
neighbours but with
fantastic views of the city.
Plagued by very strong
winds and problems with
pollution, fumes, dust and
dirt. She has almost no
time to devote to
gardening and an
underdeveloped interest in
plants. Would be willing to
learn if the garden was
not too overwhelming.

What She Wants
To party hard and garden
very little. A space for
entertaining, sunbathing
(preferably naked) –
somewhere tranquil to
escape city life. Plenty of
seating and somewhere
to eat.

What She Needs
A beginner's garden, lots
of hard landscaping, some
good well-chosen plants to
spark an embryonic fancy
to garden. Use of bright
colours to explode the
myth of gardens being
restrained and staid.

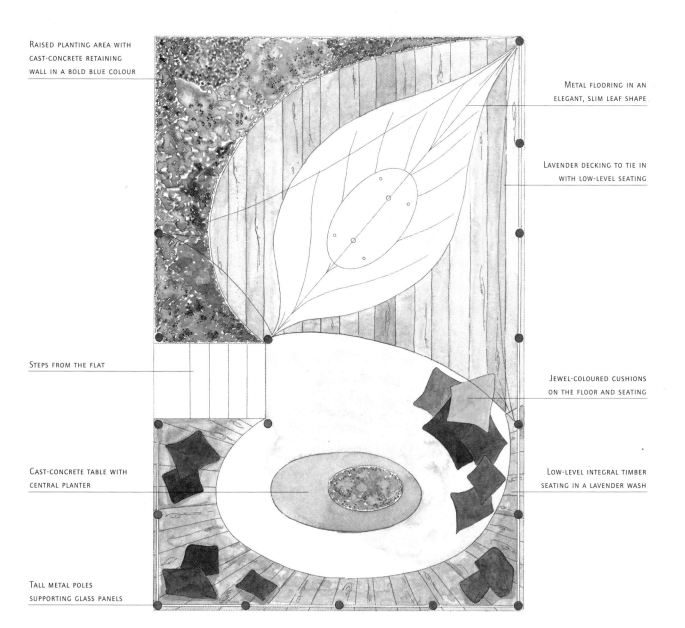

RAISED PLANTING AREA WITH
CAST-CONCRETE RETAINING
WALL IN A BOLD BLUE COLOUR

METAL FLOORING IN AN
ELEGANT, SLIM LEAF SHAPE

LAVENDER DECKING TO TIE IN
WITH LOW-LEVEL SEATING

STEPS FROM THE FLAT

JEWEL-COLOURED CUSHIONS
ON THE FLOOR AND SEATING

CAST-CONCRETE TABLE WITH
CENTRAL PLANTER

LOW-LEVEL INTEGRAL TIMBER
SEATING IN A LAVENDER WASH

TALL METAL POLES
SUPPORTING GLASS PANELS

shaded by an asymmetric canopy of sail canvas stretched between four of the blue poles, giving shelter to the diners from sun and rain.

The garden is essentially a party venue. With plenty of permanent seating it is the perfect place for lounging on Sunday afternoons, and the under-seat lighting will give a soft and subtle glow to the whole roof, making it as enjoyable a place at night as it is in the day.

TRANSLATION TO OTHER DESIGNS

The awning would be a fantastic feature in any style of garden. Altering the materials can give it an altogether different feel. You could have thick bamboo poles and a cotton canopy, or wooden posts with a striped awning. The posts need not be permanently erected. If you choose to rest them on the ground, you will need guy ropes to get tension on the canopy. Try different shapes: squares are easiest. It is a good alternative to a pergola, easier to construct and allow good light levels underneath while giving shade and shelter.

Cast concrete, as used for the table and retaining walls, is a most versatile and under-used material. With simple shuttering you can cast any shape you require very inexpensively, especially if you mix by hand, although I would recommend a ready-mixed delivery for an even consistency. Once set, the shuttering is removed and the concrete can be painted any colour you wish.

Lighting in a garden enables it to be used after dark and it is especially important in a party garden like this. Inserting the lights into seating or walls so that it is set flush gives an unobtrusive feature with a subtle glow at night. This type of lighting could also be set into decking so that the light is under your feet.

A City Roof Garden

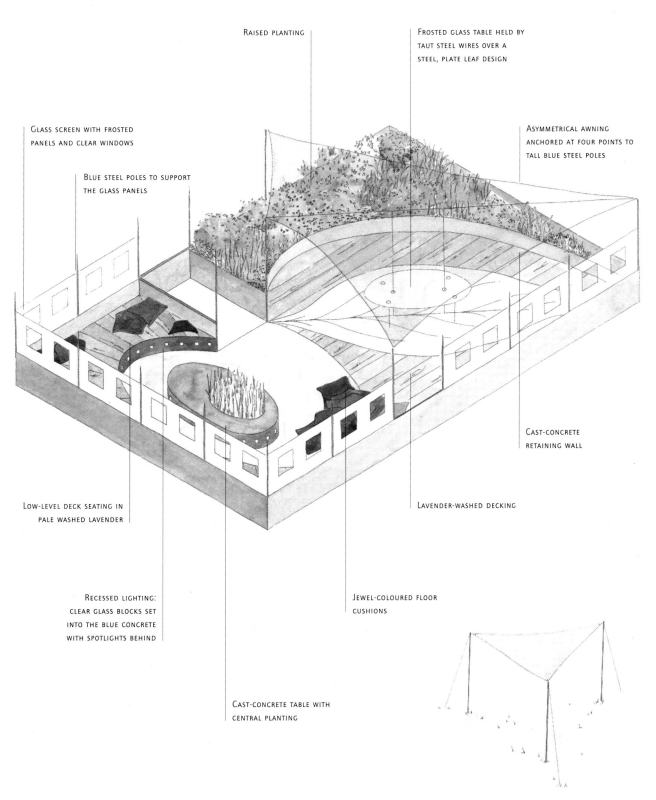

RAISED PLANTING

FROSTED GLASS TABLE HELD BY
TAUT STEEL WIRES OVER A
STEEL, PLATE LEAF DESIGN

GLASS SCREEN WITH FROSTED
PANELS AND CLEAR WINDOWS

ASYMMETRICAL AWNING
ANCHORED AT FOUR POINTS TO
TALL BLUE STEEL POLES

BLUE STEEL POLES TO SUPPORT
THE GLASS PANELS

CAST-CONCRETE
RETAINING WALL

LOW-LEVEL DECK SEATING IN
PALE WASHED LAVENDER

LAVENDER-WASHED DECKING

RECESSED LIGHTING:
CLEAR GLASS BLOCKS SET
INTO THE BLUE CONCRETE
WITH SPOTLIGHTS BEHIND

JEWEL-COLOURED FLOOR
CUSHIONS

CAST-CONCRETE TABLE WITH
CENTRAL PLANTING

AN ORGANIC VEGETABLE GARDEN

Who They Are
HOME
Victorian, three-bedroom, brick, terrace house.

OCCUPATION
Couple, both working full-time.

CHILDREN
None.

STYLE
Traditional and sympathetic to the property – they have restored the house to its original state. They love food and cooking.

TIME
Both are passionate gardeners who will devote their spare evenings and weekends to producing organic vegetables. They can spend an average of twelve hours per week between them on the garden.

This is a garden to complement a traditional, Victorian, brick house. The young owners are keen to produce everything they can for themselves in an organic way, but they like to sit outside, to eat alfresco and to be surrounded by plants that look good as well as taste good.

This garden gives them a large circular brick terrace with room enough for a table and six chairs. The terrace is encompassed by a small water rill with its source behind a large wooden bench on the south fence. Constructed of large woven willow hurdles, the fence is used as a frame to grow fan-trained figs and cordon fruit trees. The water appears from under the bench in a narrow terracotta gully and flows to the terrace, divides into two and rejoins again to disappear into a hidden reservoir next to the herb bed. It is narrow enough to step over but large enough to give the sound and sparkle of running water. The terrace has dappled shade provided by a slender metal dome heavily laden with grape vines and decorative gourds planted in large terracotta pots.

The four productive beds are circular in shape, bordered with brick on edge to give access to every part of each one. A central circle, also of brick, surrounds a 2m- (6½ft-) high willow obelisk suitable for training climbing vegetables and decorative sweet peas.

On the opposite side to the bench is a herb garden, which produces exquisite scents, flower for beauty and foliage for cooking and preserving.

The far end of the garden is divided off by espalier pear and apple trees in a curve that echoes the circular terracotta beds. This disguises the strawberry and raspberry beds, compost heaps and cold frames. Central to the top third of the garden is the glasshouse for tender vegetables, in brick and duck-egg-

What They Have
A very old garden, previously looked after by an elderly couple, west-facing, full of old overgrown plants. Although both work full-time, they are full of enthusiasm and are willing to work weekends.

What They Want
They have an evangelical need to live organically and self-sufficiently from their garden, growing vegetables, herbs, fruit. Passionate foodies, they want to try unusual varieties, yet don't want to sacrifice everything to vegetables – they want colour and vibrancy, a garden that is bold and quite brash.

What They Need
Not to take on too much; to learn crop rotation on an easy-to-use four-bed system. Disused areas for recycling, compost, water collection.

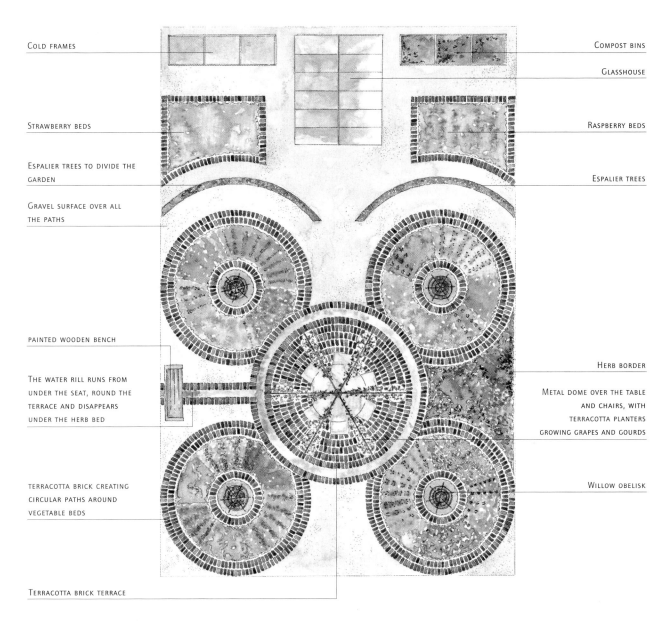

COLD FRAMES

COMPOST BINS

GLASSHOUSE

STRAWBERRY BEDS

RASPBERRY BEDS

ESPALIER TREES TO DIVIDE THE
GARDEN

ESPALIER TREES

GRAVEL SURFACE OVER ALL
THE PATHS

PAINTED WOODEN BENCH

HERB BORDER

THE WATER RILL RUNS FROM
UNDER THE SEAT, ROUND THE
TERRACE AND DISAPPEARS
UNDER THE HERB BED

METAL DOME OVER THE TABLE
AND CHAIRS, WITH
TERRACOTTA PLANTERS
GROWING GRAPES AND GOURDS

TERRACOTTA BRICK CREATING
CIRCULAR PATHS AROUND
VEGETABLE BEDS

WILLOW OBELISK

TERRACOTTA BRICK TERRACE

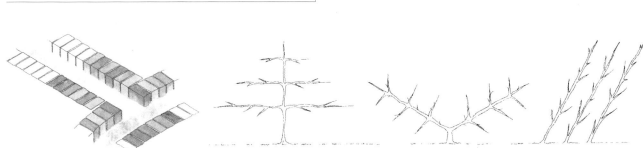

Planting List

FRUIT TREES AND SOFT FRUIT
Malus domestica (apples)
'Bramley's Seedling'
'Discovery'
'Spartan'
'Tydeman's Late Orange'

Pyrus communis (pears)
'Conference'
'Doyenné du Comice'
'Onward'
'Williams' Bon Chrétien'

Raspberries/tayberries
Strawberries
Grape vines in pots

HERBS
Allium schoenoprasum
(chive)
Artemisia dracunculus
(French tarragon)
Foeniculum vulgare
(fennel)
Laurus nobilis (bay)
Melissa officinalis
(lemon balm)
Mentha suaveolens
(apple mint)
Origanum vulgare
(oregano)
Petroselinum crispum
(parsley)
Rosmarinus officinalis
(rosemary)
Salvia officinalis (sage)
Thymus vulgaris (thyme)

blue wood. A vista through the metal dome to the house leads the eye to the glasshouse. The addition of two large water butts to collect all the rain water from the roof will probably provide enough water to satisfy the garden for most of the year.

This scheme fulfils the couple's need to turn their entire plot over to produce in order to satisfy their desire to live organically, but also allows them to have a garden that is ornamental and beautiful: the best of both worlds.

TRANSLATION TO OTHER DESIGNS

The metal dome is a feature that will sit easily over any circular terrace or at the junction of paths. Not something you can easily buy off the peg, it will need to be custom-made by your local blacksmith and should be galvanized for long life. It can then be grown with a variety of climbers or trees, from clematis to cordon apples. A word of warning: don't make it too small or you will lose the impact.

Espalier trees are a fantastic way to introduce fruit into your garden. They are particularly good at producing heavy crops on the sideways-facing branches. They can be used to create a screen, as in this design, or against a boundary if space is at a premium. You will be rewarded by blossom, foliage and fruit.

The rill around the terrace can be interpreted in your own design to follow just about any shape you desire. It could be as narrow as 30cm (1ft) wide, so would be a good choice in a garden that is short of space, and could be combined with a pond for a really spectacular finish. Rills are a great favourite with children for sailing paper boats.

COMPANION PLANTS
Calendula officinalis
(marigolds)
Ruta graveolens (rue)
Tropaeolum majus
(nasturtiums)

WILLOW OBELISKS
Runner beans

FAN-TRAINED FIG
Ficus carica 'Brown Turkey'

CORDON PLUM
Prunus domestica 'Victoria'

VEGETABLE BEDS
Bed 1
Asparagus/gooseberries,
annual herbs/salads
Bed 2
Peas, beans, onions, leeks,
celery, radish
Bed 3
Cabbage, cauliflower,
spinach, broccoli
Bed 4
Potatoes, parsnips,
celeriac, carrots

GLASSHOUSE
For raising tomatoes,
cucumbers and peppers;
also seedlings for outside
beds.

An Organic Vegetable Garden

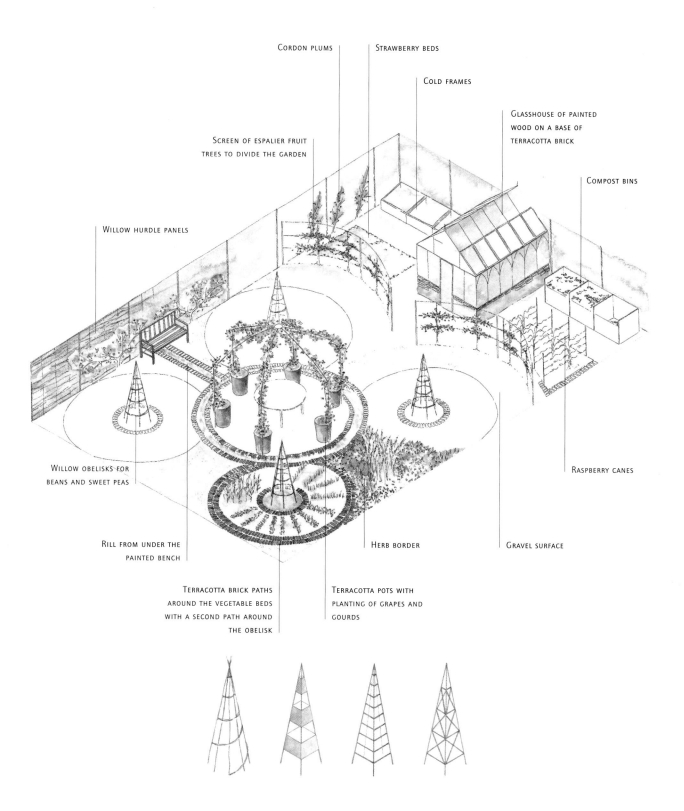

CORDON PLUMS

STRAWBERRY BEDS

COLD FRAMES

GLASSHOUSE OF PAINTED
WOOD ON A BASE OF
TERRACOTTA BRICK

SCREEN OF ESPALIER FRUIT
TREES TO DIVIDE THE GARDEN

COMPOST BINS

WILLOW HURDLE PANELS

WILLOW OBELISKS FOR
BEANS AND SWEET PEAS

RASPBERRY CANES

RILL FROM UNDER THE
PAINTED BENCH

HERB BORDER

GRAVEL SURFACE

TERRACOTTA BRICK PATHS
AROUND THE VEGETABLE BEDS
WITH A SECOND PATH AROUND
THE OBELISK

TERRACOTTA POTS WITH
PLANTING OF GRAPES AND
GOURDS

A GARDEN FOR THE SENSES

Who They Are

HOME
Rendered house with terracotta roof in a semi-rural area on the edge of a village.

OCCUPATION
He works full-time, she works part-time as an artist.

CHILDREN
Grown up and left home.

STYLE
Very traditional. House is pretty and quite cottage-like in decor. They embrace antiques and wouldn't have reproduction; love quality.

TIME
He will not work on the garden although will sit out in it. She is very keen and prepared to devote a day (about six hours) every week to gardening.

Enter the garden through double doors into the Box Garden, a geometric pattern in low box hedging with pyramid topiary in square lead containers at the edge. The ground is covered with a honey-coloured small gravel, which completes the crisp and neat look of this first garden room.

A break in the dividing yew hedge leads you down the main vista into the second garden room, the Scented Garden. The surface underfoot changes to random York stone paving running down the centre of two wide borders. These are filled with a riot of roses and lavender in shades of pink and mauve along with eight oak obelisks 2m (6½ft) high and draped with pink sweet peas. This room is an assault on the nose – the blooms are all laden with scent and shocking colour. The York path culminates in a terrace suitable for a table and chairs or even a summer house. The side wall is covered in purple wisteria, picking up the colour theme from the beds. This entire garden is lit by glass candle lanterns that appear on spikes from between the roses, giving a magical feel at night. During winter when all the blooms have died away, the obelisks become sculptural features in their own right, not just in a supporting role.

A small low archway in the hedge tempts you into the Woodland Garden, with bark chippings underfoot and below a dense canopy of trees. This garden room feels dark, calm and moist, with drifts of bulbs appearing from beneath the bark. It has a musty, warm and woody smell, and is a perfect place to retreat on a hot summer's day.

The sound of running water calls you through another small archway in the hedge and you emerge in the bright Water Garden. A large white metal bench overlooks a pond with three water spouts surrounded by terracotta tiles on edge, with gravel, in a shape that echoes the Box Garden. The view from

What They Have
South-facing plot, very boring, with a lawn and edge border. Hot and dry with extremely poor sandy soil, so drains easily. She has always had a passion for horticulture and can devote time to gardening.

What They Want
An area to paint/sculpt, inspiration from pockets of each colour scheme within the planting to provide different areas with different environments to suit her moods. Cat owner who needs spots for beloved moggies.

What They Need
To create variations in the landscape to allow development of different coloured areas, smaller eco-systems with individual environmental conditions. Lots of seating. Use of light, both natural and artificial, very important.

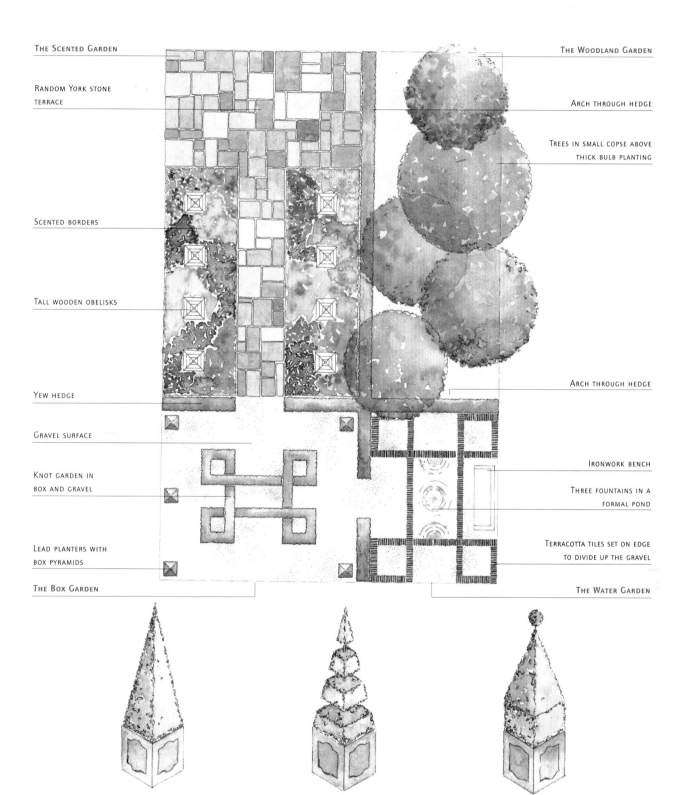

THE SCENTED GARDEN

RANDOM YORK STONE
TERRACE

SCENTED BORDERS

TALL WOODEN OBELISKS

YEW HEDGE

GRAVEL SURFACE

KNOT GARDEN IN
BOX AND GRAVEL

LEAD PLANTERS WITH
BOX PYRAMIDS

THE BOX GARDEN

THE WOODLAND GARDEN

ARCH THROUGH HEDGE

TREES IN SMALL COPSE ABOVE
THICK BULB PLANTING

ARCH THROUGH HEDGE

IRONWORK BENCH

THREE FOUNTAINS IN A
FORMAL POND

TERRACOTTA TILES SET ON EDGE
TO DIVIDE UP THE GRAVEL

THE WATER GARDEN

Planting List

BOX GARDEN
Buxus sempervirens (box)

SCENTED GARDEN
Allium cristophii
Allium 'Globemaster'
Lathyrus odoratus
(sweet pea)
Lavandula angustifolia
'Hidcote' (lavender)
Lavandula stoechas
(French lavender)
Rosa 'Constance Spry'
(rose)
Rosa 'Eglantyne' (rose)
Rosa 'Fragrant Memories'
(rose)
Rosa 'Gertrude Jekyll'
(rose)
Rosa 'Heritage' (rose)
Tulipa 'Greuze'
Wisteria sinensis

WOODLAND GARDEN
Trees
Acer pensylvanicum
(striped maple)
Cercis siliquastrum
(Judas tree)
Prunus 'Shirotae'
(flowering cherry)
Sorbus aria 'Lutescens'
(whitebeam)
Sorbus cashmiriana
(rowan)

Convallaria majalis
(Lily-of-the-valley)
Cyclamen hederifolium
(ivy-leaved cyclamen)
Galanthus nivalis
(snowdrop)
Hedera helix (ivy)
Helleborus niger
(Christmas rose)

HEDGE
Taxus baccata (yew)

the bench leads you back through an elegant doorway to the start of your journey.

Each room within the garden gives a different feel, from the cool restraint of the Box Garden to the lush dampness of the woodland. There is a place in the garden to satisfy every emotion.

TRANSLATION TO OTHER DESIGNS

Division of the garden into rooms can be achieved even in quite a limited space, giving the element of surprise to a design. If your garden is small, use lower hedges or trellis for division, but don't be afraid of using a large scale: bold is better than timid. Use the one-third: two-thirds rule (see page 14) when deciding how to divide your garden, along with ensuring that windows from the house will have good vistas. Make use of each room by giving it a different theme or atmosphere – there is no point in dividing a space into compartments and then making them all the same.

The line of obelisks in the border can be used in any style of garden. By changing the colour of the wood you can adapt the look to enhance your own scheme. If wood is too solid, try woven willow or metal. Obelisks give instant height to a new scheme while the garden develops and they have an excellent sculptural quality in winter.

If you have a group of trees similar to the one in this garden, the grass underneath will often be poor, not to mention difficult to mow, so cordon off the area with a hedge or Tanalised board edges and cover with a surface of bark chippings. It gives a natural look, is an inexpensive covering and is great for underplanting with bulbs. This makes an excellent play area for children: they love being under a canopy of trees and the bark surface is quite safe if they fall. Don't worry about the bulbs – they will recover from little feet.

SUMMER IN
THE SCENTED GARDEN:
A RIOT OF PERFUME,
COLOUR AND SPLENDOUR;
WISTERIA GROWN ON
THE BOUNDARY

AREA FOR TABLE AND
CHAIRS FOR OUTSIDE DINING
OR ROOM FOR A SMALL
SUMMER HOUSE

OBELISKS ARE SCULPTURAL
FEATURES DURING
THE WINTER MONTHS

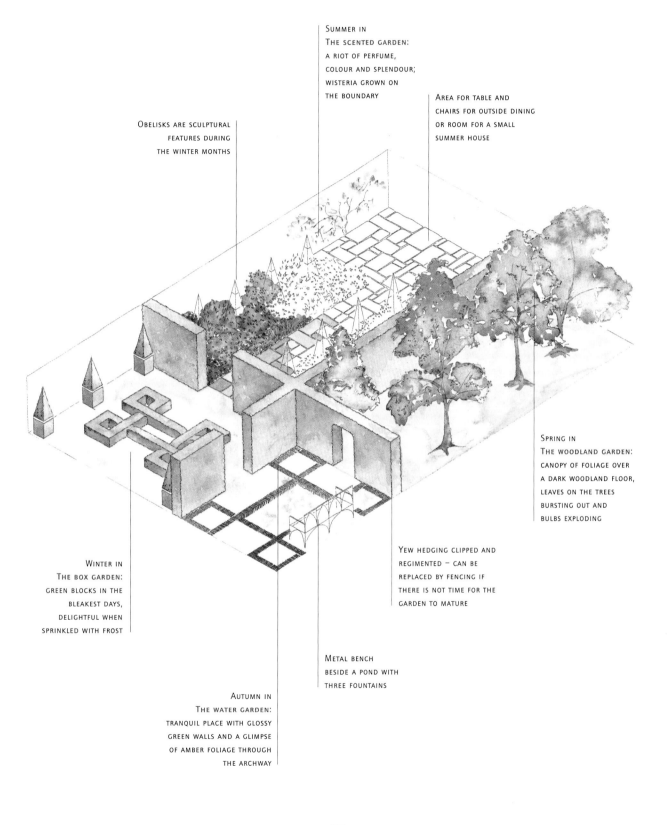

SPRING IN
THE WOODLAND GARDEN:
CANOPY OF FOLIAGE OVER
A DARK WOODLAND FLOOR,
LEAVES ON THE TREES
BURSTING OUT AND
BULBS EXPLODING

YEW HEDGING CLIPPED AND
REGIMENTED – CAN BE
REPLACED BY FENCING IF
THERE IS NOT TIME FOR THE
GARDEN TO MATURE

WINTER IN
THE BOX GARDEN:
GREEN BLOCKS IN THE
BLEAKEST DAYS,
DELIGHTFUL WHEN
SPRINKLED WITH FROST

METAL BENCH
BESIDE A POND WITH
THREE FOUNTAINS

AUTUMN IN
THE WATER GARDEN:
TRANQUIL PLACE WITH GLOSSY
GREEN WALLS AND A GLIMPSE
OF AMBER FOLIAGE THROUGH
THE ARCHWAY

A WILDLIFE GARDEN

Who They Are

HOME
Detached brick house in a semi-rural site.

OCCUPATION
He works full-time, she works part-time.

CHILDREN
One in late teens, hopefully about to leave home.

STYLE
Traditional and undesigner. They loathe anything contrived and over-done.

TIME
They love being outside and are prepared to spend four hours a week tending the garden.

This garden appears to run right into the house with no defined hard landscaping to signal proximity to the building. A door leads you from the house along a barely perceived path that is mown, into a flowering meadow. The path is edged on one side with Tanalised board, which keeps the bark-chipping mulch on the border. The mown path leads to the right through the meadow and on to a central mound of mown grass, or to the left to meet a second path next to the pond.

The pond has barely defined edges, heavily planted so that the meadow meets the water. One leg of the summer house is submerged in water.

The mown path continues in a second curve to a central circle of bark chippings, and a large tree stump makes a natural seat. The summer house is on tall legs, enabling the planting to continue underneath and create a retreat for wildlife. The walls are wattle-and-daub render with an English oak frame and a terracotta roof. Access is on two sides via a small ladder and the building is painted a soft shade of terracotta. From here you can look down on the whole garden and over the pond: it's a perfect place to observe the wildlife. As the garden looks on to open fields on two sides, there is no need for fences, allowing it to 'flow' into its surroundings. The one side that borders the neighbour's property has a low cleft-chestnut fencing to mark the boundary.

There is a mixture of flowers and foliage along with five trees to attract all sorts of animals, birds and insects. There are also nest boxes for birds in all the trees and hedgehog houses under the foliage. A large pile of logs is left in the far corner to provide more habitats.

What They Have
Detached house with solar panels and very ordinary garden in countryside; pastoral views. Both are keen ornithologists, wildlife lovers, and have lots of time to spend outside.

What They Want
A spectacular garden, but without a 'designer' look. It should incorporate lots of natural materials, be sympathetic to the countryside and be packed with plants. The garden should melt into its surroundings.

What They Need
Space to enjoy their surroundings; a building outside to use for wildlife watching; water in abundance. A garden of calm and tranquillity.

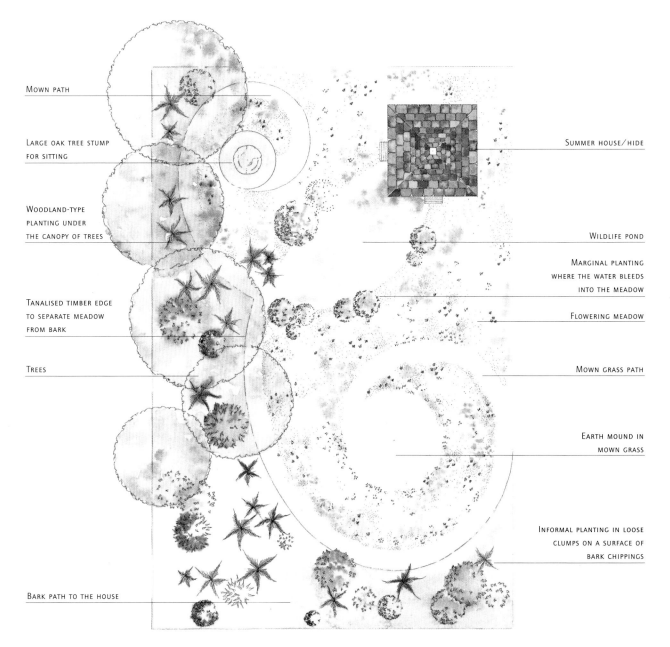

MOWN PATH

LARGE OAK TREE STUMP
FOR SITTING

WOODLAND-TYPE
PLANTING UNDER
THE CANOPY OF TREES

TANALISED TIMBER EDGE
TO SEPARATE MEADOW
FROM BARK

TREES

BARK PATH TO THE HOUSE

SUMMER HOUSE/HIDE

WILDLIFE POND

MARGINAL PLANTING
WHERE THE WATER BLEEDS
INTO THE MEADOW

FLOWERING MEADOW

MOWN GRASS PATH

EARTH MOUND IN
MOWN GRASS

INFORMAL PLANTING IN LOOSE
CLUMPS ON A SURFACE OF
BARK CHIPPINGS

Planting List

WATER PLANTING
Callitriche palustris
Gunnera manicata
Matteuccia struthiopteris
(ostrich fern)
Mentha aquatica
(water mint)
Myosotis scorpioides
(forget-me-not)
Primula florindae
(giant yellow cowslip)
Trollius europaeus
(globe flower)

MEADOW
*Chrysanthemum
leucanthemum*
(oxeye daisy)
Fritillaria meleagris
(snake's head fritillary)
Geranium pratense
(meadow cranesbill)
Ranunculus acris
(meadow buttercup)
Rumex acetosa
(common sorrel)

TREES
Aesculus hippocastanum
(horse chestnut)
Corylus avellana (hazel)
Ilex aquifolium (holly)
Juglans regia (walnut)
Malus 'Veitch's Scarlet'
(apple)

TRANSLATION TO OTHER DESIGNS

Allowing your lawn to run riot and having to mow only twice a year is a very appealing idea and enables you to grow fantastic meadow flowers. You can put over your entire lawn to meadow, though I favour mowing a pattern into it. A simple snail-shell design like this one is easily done, or you might like to try concentric squares or random squiggles. Children love this type of feature, and if you are really ambitious, you can try a mown maze.

The summer house in this design is an extravaganza constructed from expensive materials and elevated on legs, but it is a feature that crowns the garden, making it more useful in inclement weather, and in a design like this where there is no other hard landscaping to pay for, it could be your only expensive item. In my opinion it's worth every penny. If you are going to buy an off-the-peg house, try to customize it to suit your design using paint to pick up a colour in your paving or planting, or if possible use a really good roofing material such as oak shingles, thatch or tiles. If you use tiles, make sure the building is suitable to hold the weight.

GARDEN
Buddleja davidii
(butterfly bush)
Cotoneaster
Digitalis purpurea
(foxglove)
Lonicera xylosteum
(fly honeysuckle)
Polygonatum × *hybridum*
(Solomon's seal)
Polystichum setiferum
(soft shield fern)
Rosa rugosa (rose)

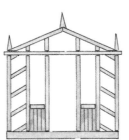
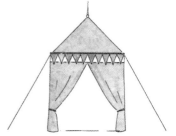

ORNAMENTAL TREES

LARGE TRUNK FOR USE AS
A SEAT

CLEFT-CHESTNUT FENCE

SUMMER HOUSE ON STILTS,
ONE LEG IN THE WILDLIFE
POND. CONSTRUCTED OF
GREEN OAK AND PLASTER
RENDER IN FADED
TERRACOTTA, WITH A ROOF OF
RECLAIMED TERRACOTTA
PANTILES

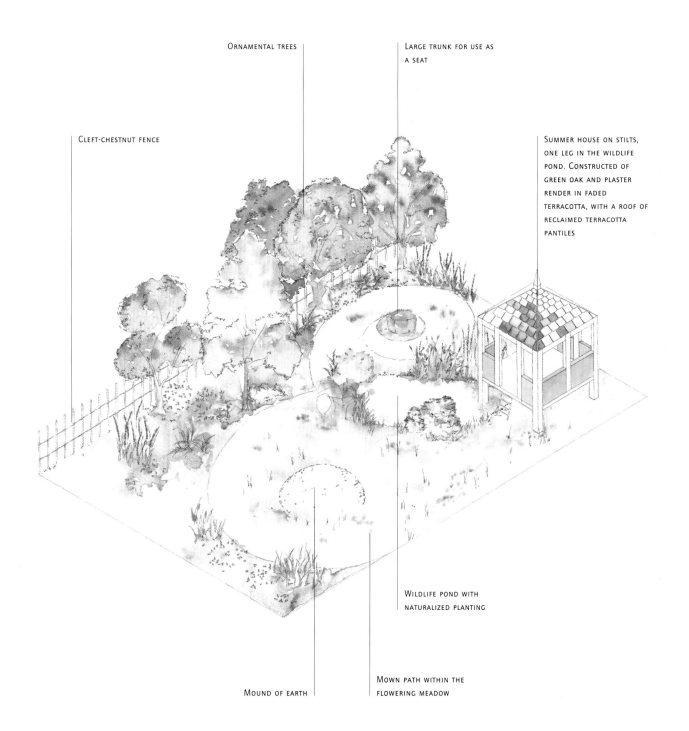

WILDLIFE POND WITH
NATURALIZED PLANTING

MOUND OF EARTH

MOWN PATH WITHIN THE
FLOWERING MEADOW

A COASTAL GARDEN

Who He Is
HOME
Individual detached
modern dwelling with
spectacular views and
no neighbours.

OCCUPATION
Single man working full-
time from home office.

CHILDREN
None.

STYLE
He loves the unusual,
revels in being different; is
very fond of the coast and
could not live without the
sea. Minimal decor in
house; no mess, very tidy.

TIME
Although a full-time
worker, he is based at
home and is prepared to
commit four hours per
week to the garden.

Entering the top terrace from the house brings you on to a deck stained a faded duck-egg-blue. In the deck is a recessed seating area, the two steps down creating an amphitheatre with a base surface of pale, fine gravel. There is enough room for a table and chairs, although the steps themselves provide seats for lounging on. The area is also protected by a privet hedge planted in a flush wooden container along the edge of the level change, giving protection against the wind. This top deck is bordered by low decorative fencing in a shade of blue-green to complement the deck, which is softened by huge terracotta urns, some planted with agave.

Small wooden steps lead you on to the second level, with a retaining wall of chunky wooden sleepers, sand-blasted to enhance the grain. This level has a surface of gravel with random planting and a plinth for a large sculpture.

More steps take you on to a further level of gravel, and descending a final flight you arrive on the lower terrace. This area is of deck with a central shape holding smooth white dinosaur-egg cobbles and several huge boulders large enough to sit on while admiring the view out to sea. This lower deck is covered by three evergreen oaks helping to break the wind flow and providing shade in summer.

The final level is one step up to an area of purple-blue slate paddlestones with masses of architectural random planting in blues and yellow: the perfect place to sling a hammock. The final level changes are also managed in chunky wood, but set horizontally with heavy vertical posts to resemble old groynes.

What He Has
A plot facing the east
coast with salt-laden
winds and magnificent sea
views. He is a very keen
gardener with a taste for
the unusual.

What He Wants
A garden that reflects
his personality, with
sculptures and odd plants.
He is prepared to look
after the garden carefully
and would like tender
plants. He also wants a
venue for outside dining.

What He Needs
A garden that will cope
with most difficult
conditions, sympathetic
with the coast and
sea without looking
obviously themed.

A Coastal Garden

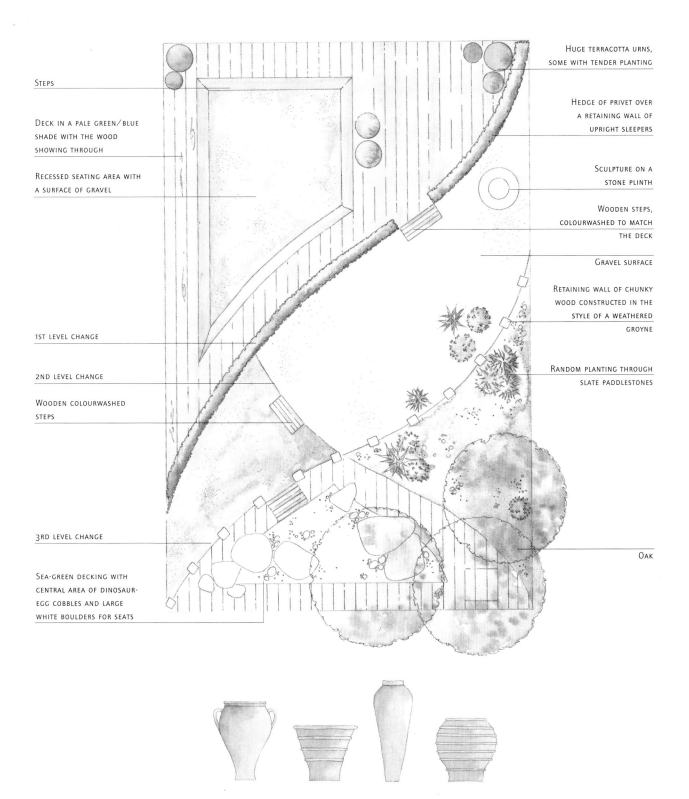

STEPS

DECK IN A PALE GREEN/BLUE
SHADE WITH THE WOOD
SHOWING THROUGH

RECESSED SEATING AREA WITH
A SURFACE OF GRAVEL

1ST LEVEL CHANGE

2ND LEVEL CHANGE

WOODEN COLOURWASHED
STEPS

3RD LEVEL CHANGE

SEA-GREEN DECKING WITH
CENTRAL AREA OF DINOSAUR-
EGG COBBLES AND LARGE
WHITE BOULDERS FOR SEATS

HUGE TERRACOTTA URNS,
SOME WITH TENDER PLANTING

HEDGE OF PRIVET OVER
A RETAINING WALL OF
UPRIGHT SLEEPERS

SCULPTURE ON A
STONE PLINTH

WOODEN STEPS,
COLOURWASHED TO MATCH
THE DECK

GRAVEL SURFACE

RETAINING WALL OF CHUNKY
WOOD CONSTRUCTED IN THE
STYLE OF A WEATHERED
GROYNE

RANDOM PLANTING THROUGH
SLATE PADDLESTONES

OAK

Planting List

Agave americana
Agave parryi
Carex (sedge)
Cordyline (club palm)
Eryngium agavifolium
(sea holly)
Eryngium giganteum
(sea holly)
Eryngium × tripartitum
(sea holly)
Ligustrum ovalifolium
(privet)
Phormium tenax
(New Zealand flax)
Quercus ilex
(evergreen oak)
Rosmarinus officinalis
(rosemary)
Sempervivum montanum
(house leek)
Sisyrinchium striatum

TRANSLATION TO OTHER DESIGNS

The recessed seating area could be constructed in any type of material, although decking is the easiest. Level changes give a garden interest and provide a large amount of permanent seating and a place to congregate. They are particularly easy to create if, as in this garden, you have a site with more than one level, but it is possible to do this type of design on any plot if you don't mind digging.

Boulders as seats, while not comfortable for a long period of lounging, are great for a simple, inexpensive loitering point. You can use any type of rock, though a smooth top is preferable, and when they aren't being used as seats they have a sculptural quality, especially if lit at night. Remember to keep to odd numbers – three, five or seven will look best – and to vary the sizes. The occasional small rock at the base of a large one will make it look more at home and natural.

The outline shape of this garden is an easy one to try, especially if you are designing a garden in an odd-shaped plot, such as one that tapers to a point. Draw bold curves on your plan from one corner point to the opposite corner of your house and then fan out the lines to give areas that can be used for terrace, bed or lawn. A line from the opposite corners crossing these, also in a curved sweep, will divide the garden further.

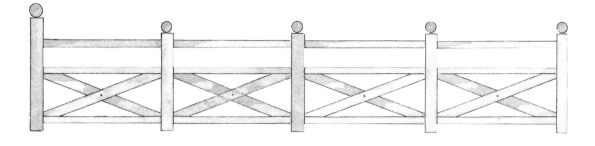

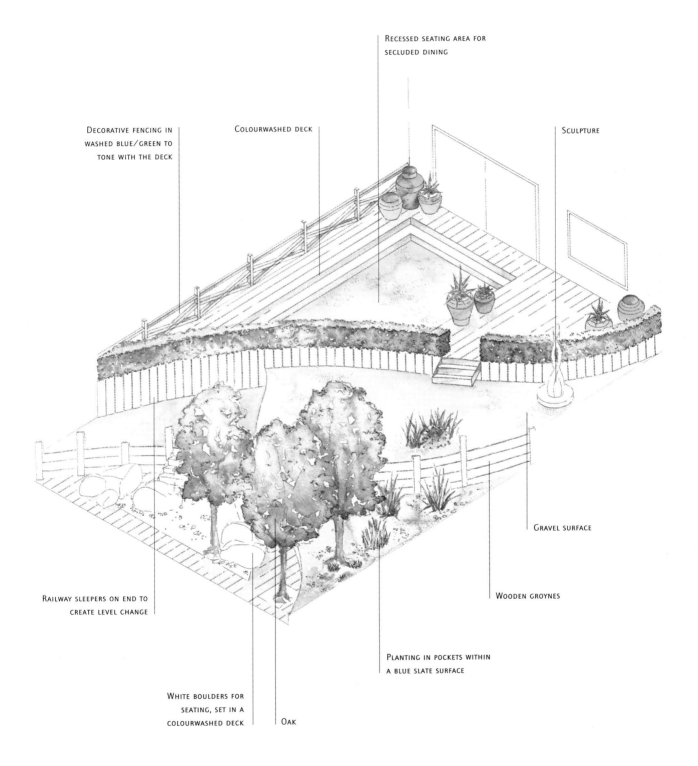

RECESSED SEATING AREA FOR
SECLUDED DINING

DECORATIVE FENCING IN
WASHED BLUE/GREEN TO
TONE WITH THE DECK

COLOURWASHED DECK

SCULPTURE

RAILWAY SLEEPERS ON END TO
CREATE LEVEL CHANGE

GRAVEL SURFACE

WOODEN GROYNES

PLANTING IN POCKETS WITHIN
A BLUE SLATE SURFACE

WHITE BOULDERS FOR
SEATING, SET IN A
COLOURWASHED DECK

OAK

A GARDEN FOR THE DISABLED

This garden exudes elegance and restraint. As you enter the central path of deep blue-grey granite setts you are led past two chamomile lawns, one on either side. The path then divides into two further symmetrical routes around the garden. These travel first towards a square terrace with a central stone urn, then turn to travel between a row of five erect beech trees in single row and a border of shrubs and perennials, all with a yellow flowering theme.

The paths meet again at the top of the garden at another small chamomile lawn recessed into a large raised bed. The bed is constructed of chunky oak beams and contains low-growing evergreens and five tall columnar junipers. The seating area gives you a perfect view back down the plot into the sunken garden. A sett ramp takes you down to an area of pressed gravel, suitable for wheelchair use. The retaining walls are also of oak.

Changing the garden levels by travelling down as well as up adds a great deal of interest to a flat plot and allows a wheelchair user access to maintain this garden.

What They Have
South-west-facing traditional garden; lots of herbaceous borders, masses of pots and bedding schemes.

What They Want
A garden with full wheelchair access that will allow them to enjoy gardening without it being a burden to them. Keeping lots of colour with a very traditional look and retaining the lawn are important to them.

What They Need
Raised beds with integrated watering systems for ease of maintenance. Somewhere to sit and relax. An alternative to lawn and annuals.

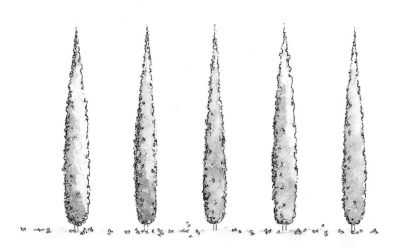

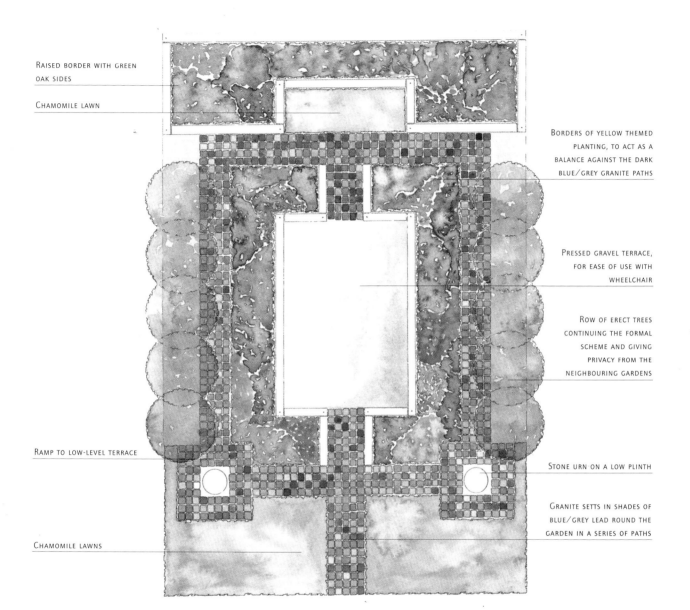

RAISED BORDER WITH GREEN
OAK SIDES

CHAMOMILE LAWN

BORDERS OF YELLOW THEMED
PLANTING, TO ACT AS A
BALANCE AGAINST THE DARK
BLUE/GREY GRANITE PATHS

PRESSED GRAVEL TERRACE,
FOR EASE OF USE WITH
WHEELCHAIR

ROW OF ERECT TREES
CONTINUING THE FORMAL
SCHEME AND GIVING
PRIVACY FROM THE
NEIGHBOURING GARDENS

RAMP TO LOW-LEVEL TERRACE

STONE URN ON A LOW PLINTH

GRANITE SETTS IN SHADES OF
BLUE/GREY LEAD ROUND THE
GARDEN IN A SERIES OF PATHS

CHAMOMILE LAWNS

Planting List

TWO MAIN BEDS
Achillea 'Taygetea'
(yarrow)
Alchemilla mollis
(lady's mantle)
Angelica archangelica
Corylus avellana
'Contorta' (corkscrew
hazel)
Fritillaria imperialis
(crown imperial fritillary)
Fritillaria pallidiflora
(fritillary)
Hemerocallis
'Marion Vaughn' (day lily)
Origanum vulgare
'Aureum'
(golden marjoram)
Phlomis russeliana
Pulsatilla vernalis
Solidago 'Laurin'
(golden rod)
Trollius europaeus
(globe flower)
Verbascum olympicum

TREES
Fagus sylvatica 'Dawyck'
(beech)

TREE UNDERPLANTING
Erythronium 'Pagoda'

END RAISED BEDS
Hedera helix (ivy)
Humulus lupulus 'Aureus'
(golden hop)
Juniperus scopulorum
'Skyrocket'

TRANSLATION TO OTHER DESIGNS

Changing the ground levels of your design is not only applicable when you are dealing with a wheelchair-access garden. It is extremely useful for adding interest and a feeling of enclosure and intimacy. Admittedly it means moving a huge quantity of earth, but if you can balance any drop in level with a rise in level, you will be able to reuse in the raised area most of the soil that is dug out. Never leave a wall made just from earth, unless the angle of the slope is very shallow, or as soon as it rains your earth wall will disappear.

Using one genus of tree repeated in a line of planting, such as these beeches and junipers, makes a bold statement in your planting scheme. Don't be afraid to line trees up: formal schemes cry out for avenues. They look best on either side of a path or, as in this case, either side of a garden. It's generally advisable to use a genus that has a defined shape, although there is no reason why you could not have a line of weeping trees instead of fastigiate ones. Bear in mind the width of a feature like this and allow plenty of room for growth or your path will disappear into the foliage. Choose a slim conifer or a tree that can be trimmed to leave a single straight trunk, and always line up your trees and space them accurately. If one is slightly out of line, it will look awful.

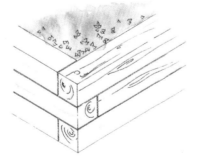

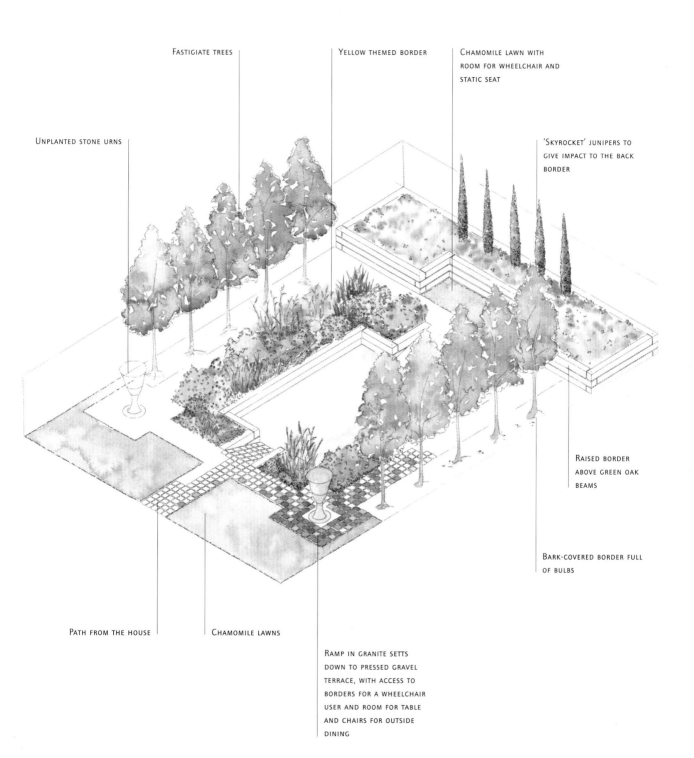

FASTIGIATE TREES

YELLOW THEMED BORDER

CHAMOMILE LAWN WITH
ROOM FOR WHEELCHAIR AND
STATIC SEAT

UNPLANTED STONE URNS

'SKYROCKET' JUNIPERS TO
GIVE IMPACT TO THE BACK
BORDER

RAISED BORDER
ABOVE GREEN OAK
BEAMS

BARK-COVERED BORDER FULL
OF BULBS

PATH FROM THE HOUSE

CHAMOMILE LAWNS

RAMP IN GRANITE SETTS
DOWN TO PRESSED GRAVEL
TERRACE, WITH ACCESS TO
BORDERS FOR A WHEELCHAIR
USER AND ROOM FOR TABLE
AND CHAIRS FOR OUTSIDE
DINING

ADAPTING THE DESIGNS

THE TRIANGULAR PLOT

Translation of the designs onto awkward-shaped gardens

Without a doubt the most difficult shape for an inexperienced designer to tackle is the triangle. It is hard to know whether to ignore the pointed corner completely or struggle to design the whole garden around that one point. There is, however, a solution that will save you all the heartache – a spiral, or part of one, has flowing lines that allow you to fill the 'fat' end of your plot with the bulk of the shape, while the tail of the spiral can taper out into the point (Diagram 1). Ammonites and snail shells provide great inspiration and demonstrate this shape in perfect use, or, if you are feeling ambitious, how about studying the galaxies?

'A Wildlife Garden' (page 136) demonstrates this use of spirals in a design. The original plan used two interlocking spirals, but there is no reason to restrict yourself; use as many as you need entwined together, and the spaces created where one line dissects another will give you organic shapes for borders, paths and terraces.

If the spirals are creating shapes that are too intricate, try simply connecting one corner of

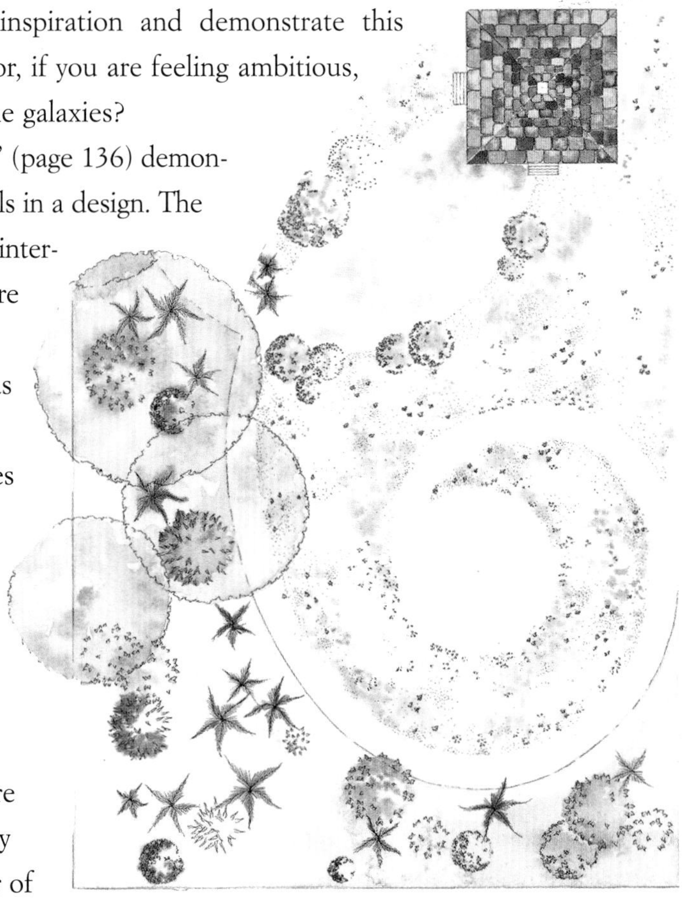

Diagram 1

your plot with another in soft sweeps; also, choose a point
approximately one-third of the way along the long boundary,
then join this point with a sweeping line to its opposite corner,
to delineate the space. You can see this in the adapted
'Coastal Garden' design (Diagram 2), which also shows the
use of a sculpture at the farthest point of the plot, drawing
the eye along the longest axis of the garden and making the
space feel much longer than it actually is.

These designs are wonderful if the look you are striving
for is soft and informal, but if what you crave is straight
lines and formal features, then the best way forward is
to separate the pointed end of the garden off from
the rest of the design. Divide the space horizontally into thirds and make the top third a
completely separate garden, using
either a hedge or fence. This
top area may be perfect for
an informal meadow,
an area of trees or
perhaps a play
space for the
children.

Diagram 2

Diagram 4

THE L-SHAPED PLOT

A garden that is viewed from more than one vantage point becomes more difficult to design, as you have to consider the layout from several angles. It will probably be possible to access the garden through more than one entrance, in which case adapting a design such as 'A Garden for the Senses' (Diagram 4) allows the viewer to walk through three different gardens.

Using geometric shapes such as squares makes negotiating corner spaces a much easier process. The natural division of the L shape into two separate arms also gives the opportunity to incorporate areas within your plot that have completely different themes.

Of course, the corner where the two designs meet will have to be sympathetically handled or it might look as if you can't decide on your garden style. The amalgamation of a section from 'A Stylish Minimal Garden' with the knot area from 'A Garden for the Senses' (Diagram 3), shows how simple it can be to join the two designs by using the individual sections of garden rather like building blocks and piecing them together to turn corners with ease; the use of pleached trees with a small archway cut through them divides the space, giving privacy to each area.

The same principles can be used for gardens that are on three or more sides of a property.

Diagram 3

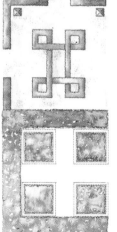

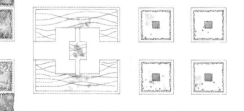

THE SQUARE COURTYARD

Surprisingly, one of the easiest ways to tackle a small square plot is by using circles. You can see from the sections of 'A Suburban Family Garden' (Diagram 5) how you can use one circle to fill the whole plot, with further concentric circles to delineate garden features, such as lawn and borders. If this is far too simple for your style, then you can use several circles that inter-lock to form one cohesive shape, such as this section from 'An Organic Vegetable Garden' (Diagram 6). I have to confess that I do favour symmetrical patterns when I am designing small square spaces – it is always pleasing to the eye to echo symme-try within a design when you find it in the garden outline.

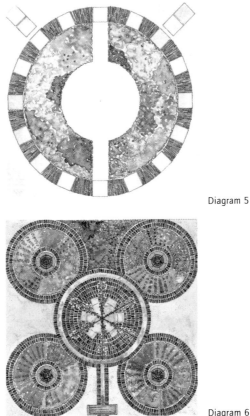

Diagram 5

Diagram 6

THE LONG, THIN PLOT

Although a long, thin garden is often presented as a problem site, I am never quite sure why, as it is one of the easiest garden shapes to deal with. Garden designers are forever talking about dividing space into rooms, and to do this in a long, thin plot is relatively easy. The one important rule to remember is to use 'the golden mean' and divide the space into thirds (see page 14); that way the garden will always have pleasing proportions.

It is necessary within a long, narrow space to give the viewer a reason to make the journey to the end of your garden. This is, of course, essential in any plot, but particularly so in a narrow area where the garden can often easily be viewed from one vantage point. A reward at the end of the plot, such as a bench, a sculpture or a water feature, will make the viewer curious enough to walk there to investigate.

You can see how this would work with the adaptation of the 'Garden for the Senses' design (Diagram 8). A sculpture positioned at the far end of the garden, nestling underneath the trees, will entice the viewer to travel through the water garden and through the gap in the hedge to emerge in the woodland area.

The adaptation of 'A Garden for the Disabled' (Diagram 7) shows another way in which you can make the most of a long, narrow space. A path that takes a route around the garden will take the viewer on a journey during which you can reveal different facets of the plot along the way. The planting in the central island border obscures the view of the whole garden, adding to the feeling of discovery.

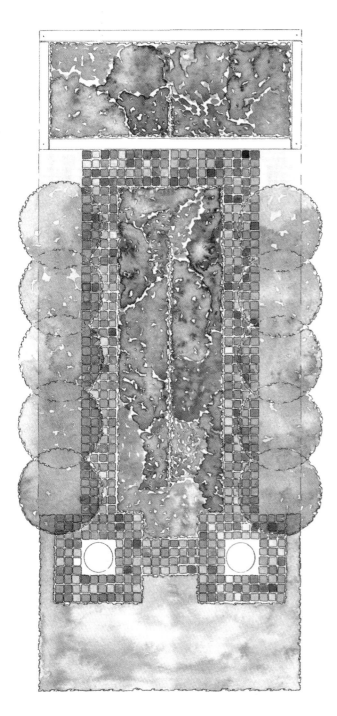

Diagram 7

Diagram 8

PRACTICAL POINTS

- Slope on a terrace to ensure good drainage: 1:70.

- Always make the slope away from any buildings and ensure that wherever the run of water will end up, there is free drainage.

- Minimum height of pergola or archway: 2m (6½ft).

- Ideal size of a seat: height 42cm (16½in), depth 40cm (15½in).

- Minimum border width: 1m.

- Minimum path width for two people to walk side by side, or for one to wheel a barrow: 1m.

- All timber for exterior use must be pressure-treated with preservative (Tanalised) or painted on installation with a suitable exterior-grade preservative.

- Mix to lay slabs or paving: 1 part cement to 6 parts mixed aggregate.

- Steps within a design must have a minimum tread of 45cm (17¾in) and a maximum rise of 15cm (6in). Make each step within a flight the same or you will find them difficult to use.

- For laying slabs dry, bed them onto a well-compacted layer of sand on top of a layer of compacted hardcore.

- Minimum width (or diameter) of a patio for a table and four chairs: 2.5m (8¼ft).

- Approximate coverage rates:

Bricks laid flat: 36 per m²

Bricks laid on edge: 54 per m²

1 tonne setts (100 x 100 x 100) will cover: 4m²

1 tonne pebbles 50mm deep will cover: 7m²

1 tonne gravel 50mm deep will cover: 12m²

1 tonne York stone slabs 50mm deep will cover: 7.5m²

- Boundary fences should be 2m (6½ft) high or less, unless agreed by both adjoining properties.

- Greenhouse orientation should run east to west.

SUPPLIERS' DIRECTORY

Hard Landscaping

Border Hardcore and Rockery Stone Company Ltd
Buttington Quarry
Welshpool
Powys SY21 8SZ
Tel: 01938 570375
Fax: 01938 570410
E-mail: sales@border-stone.demon.co.uk
Website: http://www.border-stone.demon.co.uk

CED Ltd
728 London Road
West Thurrock
Grays
Essex RM16 1LU
Tel: 0708 867237

Dry Stone Walling Association of Great Britain
c/o YFC Centre
National Agricultural Centre
Stoneleigh Park
Warwickshire CV8 2LG
Tel/fax: 0121 3780493

Breedon plc
Breedon-on-the-Hill
Derby DE73 1AP
Tel: 01332 862254
Fax: 01332 863149

Bradstone Home and Garden Landscaping
Hulland Ward
Ashbourne
Derbyshire DE6 3ET
Tel: 01335 372222
Fax: 01335 370079
Website: http://www.camas.com

Marshalls
Southowram
Halifax
Yorkshire HX3 9SY
Tel: 01422 306000
Fax: 01422 330185
Website: www.marshalls.co.uk/drivesandpatios

Pots

Whichford Pottery
Whichford
Nr Shipston-on-Stour
Warwickshire CV36 5PG
Tel: 01608 684416
Fax: 01608 684833
E-mail: whichfordpottery@compuserve.com

Teast Trading
Providence Place
Belle Vue Road
Wivenhoe
Essex CO7 9LE
Tel: 01206 826453
Fax: 01206 823965

Pots and Pithoi
The Barns
East Street
Turners Hill
West Sussex RH10 4QQ
Tel: 01342 714793
Fax: 01342 717090
E-mail: info@pots-and-pithoi.co.uk
Website: www.pots-and-pithoi.co.uk

Benches

Barlow Tyrie Ltd
Braintree
Essex CM7 2RN
Tel: 01376 557600
Fax: 01376 557610

Rusco
Little Faringdon Mill
Lechlade
Gloucestershire GL7 3QQ
Tel: 01367 252754
Fax: 01367 253406
E-mail: rusco@lfm.co.uk
Website: www.lfm.co.uk

Jason Griffiths Underwoodsman
Higher Tideford
Cornworthy
Totnes
Devon TQ9 7HL
Tel: 01803 712387
Fax: 01803 712388

Christopher Hartnoll
Iron Garden Furniture
Little Bray House
Brayford
Nr Barnstaple
North Devon EX32 7QG
Tel: 0598 710295

Plants

Jungle Giants
Burford House
Tenbury Wells
Worcestershire WR15 8HQ
Tel: 01584 819885
Fax: 01584 810673

Claire Austin Hardy Plants
Bowling Green Lane
Albrighton
Wolverhampton WV7 3HB
Tel: 01902 373931
Fax: 01902 372142

Mattocks Roses
Nuneham Courtenay
Oxfordshire OX44 9PY
Tel: 0345 585652
Fax: 01865 343166
Website: www.mattocks.co.uk

James Coles and Sons (Nurseries) Ltd
The Nurseries
Thurnby
Leicestershire LE7 9QB
Tel: 01162 412115
Fax: 01162 432311
E-mail: jcoles@james-coles-nurseries.co.uk
Website: james-coles-nurseries.co.uk

R. V. Roger Ltd
The Nurseries
Pickering
North Yorkshire YO18 7HG
Tel: 01751 472226
Fax: 01751 476749
E-mail: Ian@clivia.demon.co.uk

Postal Plants
Walford Heath
Shrewsbury
Shropshire SY4 2HT
Tel: 01939 291475
Fax: 01939 290743
E-mail: mail@postalplants.co.uk
Website: www.postalplants.co.uk

Reclaim Yards

Solo Park plc
Station Road
Nr Pampisford
Cambrigeshire CB2 4HB
Tel: 01223 834663
Fax: 01223 834780
E-mail: info@solopark.co.uk
Website: www.solopark.co.uk

Lassco
Mark Street
Off Paul Street
London EC2A 4ER
Tel: 0207 749 9944
Website: http:// www.lasco.co.uk

Sundries

ARCHES

Agriframes Ltd
Charlwood Road
East Grinstead
West Sussex RH19 2HP
Tel: 01342 310000
Fax: 01342 310099
E-mail: agriframes@btinternet.com
Website: www.agriframes.co.uk

DECKING

Blenheim Palace Decking
Combe
Witney
Oxfordshire OX8 8ET
Tel: 01993 881206
Fax: 01993 883156
E-mail: sales@blenheimsawmill.demon.co.uk
Website:
http://www.blenheimsawmill.demon.co.uk

GLASS BLOCKS

Luxcrete Ltd
Premier House
Disraeli Road
Park Royal
London NW10 7BT
Tel: 0208 965 7292
Fax: 0208 961 6337

LANDSCAPERS

British Association of Landscape Industries (BALI)
Landscape House
9 Henry Street
Keighley
West Yorkshire BD21 3DR
Tel: 01535 606139
Fax: 01535 610269

MIRRORS

Mirror Technology
Craswell Scientfic Ltd
Toddington
Gloucestershire GL5 45EB
Tel: 01242 621534

PLAY EQUIPMENT

Rainbow Play Systems Ltd.
Hillier Garden Centre
London Road
Windlesham
Surrey GU20 6LN
Tel: 01344 874662
Fax: 01344 874663
E-mail: sales@rainbowplay.co.uk
Website: www.rainbowplay.co.uk

WATER FEATURES

Oase (UK) Ltd.
Oase House
2 Northway
Walworth Industrial Estate
Andover
Hampshire SP10 5AZ
Tel: 01264 333225
Fax: 01264 333226
E-mail: oase.uk@btinternet.com
Website: www.oase-uk.co.uk

INDEX

Page numbers in *italic* refer to the illustrations

A

Acer palmatum 92
   A. pensylvanicum 134
Achillea 'Taygetea' 146
acid soils 94
Aesculus hippocastanum 138
Agapanthus 88
   A. 'Dorothy Palmer' 74, 78
Agave americana 142
   A. parryi 142
Alchemilla mollis 74, 76, *97*, 146
Allium cristophii 78, 134
   A. 'Globemaster' 134
   A. sphaerocephalon 19
Anemone × *hybrida* 'Honorine Jobert' 74, 78
Angelica archangelica 80, 146
Anglesey Abbey, Cambridgeshire 17
annuals 88
archways 109, 111, 155
Astrantia major 126
awnings 38, 126, *127*
azaleas 92, 94

B

bamboos 90, 113
bay trees 90
beans 41
beds, raised 34, 116, *119*, 144, *145*
beech hedges 54, 56, *56*
benches 34, *35*
bog plants 68
bougainvillea 92
boundaries *46–57*, 47–57, 112
bowers 33
box *see Buxus sempervirens*
brick: lawn edging *29*
   paths 24, *24*
   paving 31, 155
   pergolas 38
   walls 52, *52*

bubble fountains 62, 69
Buddleja davidii 138
   B. davidii 'Peace' 122
buildings 38–40, *39–40*
bulbs 84, 134
Buxus sempervirens (box) *30*, 76, 86, 88, 90, 92, 116, 118, 126, 132, 134

C

Calendula officinalis 130
Callitriche palustris 68, 138
Campanula persicifolia 122
canals *58*, 59, 60
Carex 90, 142
Ceanothus 74
Cedrus deodara 80
Ceratophyllum demersum 68
Cercis siliquastrum 134
chamomile 28, *28*, 33, 60, 144, *145*, *147*
Chatsworth, Derbyshire 17
chequer-board patios *121*, 122
chestnut trees *10*
children 69–70, 120–2
Choisya ternata 122
Chrysanthemum leucanthemum 138
Cimicifuga racemosa 68, 118
circles 107, 109, *109*, 151, *151*
citrus trees 92
city gardens 124–6, *125*, *127*
clay soils 94–6
Clematis 96, 120, *123*
   C. armandii 78, 122
   C. florida 'Sieboldii' 122
   C. 'H.F. Young' 122
   C. 'Henryi' 122
climbing plants 41, 48, 51, 111
coastal gardens 140–2, *141–3*
cobbles 30–1
Colchicum speciosum 'Album' 118
colour: boundaries 48, *49*
   containers 43
   decks 21

furniture 34, *35*
   obelisks 41
   pergolas 36
   plants 73–4
   summer houses 40
companion plants 130
compost 97
concrete 126
containers 42–4, *42–3*, *45*
contemporary gardens 90, *93*
Convallaria 90
   C. majalis 134
Cordyline 92, 142
Cornus alba 'Sibirica' 84
Corylus avellana 138
   C.a. 'Contorta' 80, *80*, 84, 122, 146
Cotoneaster 138
cottage gardens 89–90, *89*, 98
courtyards 151, *151*
Crataegus monogyna 54, 56, 122
crinkle-crankle walls 52, *52*
Crocus sieberi 'Bowles' White' 118
curves 107, 109, *109*
Cyclamen hederifolium 134
Cynara cardunculus 80
Cyperus involucratus 68

D

Daphne odora 'Aureomarginata' 126
decks 21–2, *21*, *23*, 113, 140, *141*, *143*
delphiniums 89
Dierama pendulum 68
Digitalis purpurea 78, 94, 138
   D.p. 'Alba' 90, 118
disabled, gardens for 144–6, *145–7*
drainage 95, 155

E

Echeveria 11
Echinops ritro 'Veitch's Blue' 122
Eremurus 99
   E. himalaicus 78
   E. robustus 122

Erica 94
Eryngium agavifolium 142
   E. giganteum 142
   E. × *tripartitum* 142
Erythronium 'Pagoda' 146
espaliers 128, *129*, 130, *131*
Eucalyptus niphophila 76, *76*
evergreens 82–4
eyesores, hiding 51–2

F

Fagus sylvatica 54, 56, *56*
   F.s. 'Dawyck' 80, 146
family gardens 120–2, *120–3*
feature plants 80
fences 47, 48, *49*, 50–1, *51*, 53, 54, 56, 155
Fibonacci, Leonardo 12–14, *19*, 107
Foeniculum vulgare 'Purpureum' 76
foliage plants 76, 82–4, 111
follies 38–40
formal gardens 90, *92*
fountains *59*, 62–4, *63*, 70, *133*
Fritillaria imperialis 146
   F. meleagris 78, 138
   F. pallidiflora 146
frost damage, containers 42
fruit 28, 128, *129*, 130, *131*

G

Galanthus 98
   G. nivalis 74, 78, 118, 134
Garrya elliptica 80, *80*
gates 46, 53–4, *53*, *54*
geotextile membrane 30, 111
Geranium 89
   G. endressii 126
   G. pratense 138
   G. sanguineum 'Album' 122
Gladiolus italicus 126
glass, crushed 30
golden mean 14, *19*, 152
grass paths *25*, 28
   see also lawns

gravel 24, 30, *30*, *31*, 86, *93*, 155
greenhouses 128–30, 155
Gunnera manicata 68, *69*, 76, 138

H
hammocks 36
hawthorn 54, 56, 120
Hedera helix (ivy) 48, *49*, 76, *76*,
  122, 134, 146
hedges 47, 50, 54–7, *55–7*, 86–8,
  92, 120, *121*
Helleborus niger 78, 134
Hemerocallis 'Marion Vaughn' 146
herbs 85, 128, 130
Heuchera micrantha var. *diversifolia*
  'Palace Purple' 126
holly 54, 56, 120
hollyhocks 89
hosta 90
Humulus lupulus 'Aureus' 76, *76*, 146

I
Ilex aquifolium 54, 56, 122, 138
inspiration 11–18
Iris sibirica 68, *70*
irregular plots, surveying 104, *104*
ivy *see Hedera helix*

J
Jasminum officinale 90
Juglans regia 138
Juniperus scopulorum 'Skyrocket' 80,
  146

K
knots 84–8, *85*, *87*, *133*

L
L-shaped plots 150, *150*
Lathyrus odoratus 134
Laurus nobilis 90
Lavandula (lavender) 132
  L. angustifolia 'Hidcote' 78, 86,
    88, 134

L. stoechas 134
lawns 25, 26–8, *27–9*
Leucojum vernum 118
levels, surveying 104, *105*
lighting *117*, 118, 126, *127*, 132
Ligustrum ovalifolium 56, 142
Lilium 72
  L. 'Casa Blanca' 78
lime, pleached 116, *117*, 118, *119*
liners, ponds 66
Liriodendron tulipifera 80, *80*
Liriope muscari 78, 126
long, narrow gardens 111–12, 152,
  153
Lonicera xylosteum 138

M
Mackintosh, Charles Rennie 18
Malus 'Veitch's Scarlet' 138
manure 96
marginal plants 68
marking out 108–10, *108–9*
Matteuccia struthiopteris 68, 138
mazes 84–5, 86, 138
meadows 28, *29*, 136, *137*, 138
measurements 101–2, 108
Mediterranean gardens *90*, 92
Mentha aquatica 68, 138
metal: obelisks 41
  pergolas 38
minimalist gardens *93*, 116–18,
  117–19
mirrors 52, 112, 118, *119*
modular gardens 148–53
Morris, William 17–18, *18*
Muscari armeniacum 122
mushroom compost 96
Myosotis scorpioides 68, 138

N
narrow gardens 111–12, 152, *153*
Nepeta × *faassenii* 122
noise pollution 50–1, *64*, 112–13
north-facing gardens 111

Nymphaea alba 67, 68

O
obelisks 40–1, *41*, 132, *133*, 134,
  135
Ophiopogon planiscapus
  'Nigrescens' 80, *81*
organic gardens 128–30, *129*, *131*
organic matter 95, 96–7
oriental gardens 90–2, 111
Origanum vulgare 'Aureum' 146
ovals, marking out 109

P
Papaver orientale 'Mrs Perry' 122
parterres 18, 84–6
Passiflora caerulea 122
paths 22–5, *22–5*, 86, 109, 110, 155
patios 31, 107, *121*, 122, 155
paving 30–1, *30–1*
paving slabs 24–5
pelargoniums 92
Penstemon 'Apple Blossom' 122
perennials 98
pergolas 22, *23*, 36–8, *37*, 109, 111,
  155
Perovskia atriplicifolia 'Blue Spire' 78
pH values, soil 92–4
Philadelphus 'Virginal' 78, 122
Phlomis russeliana 146
Phlox paniculata 'White Admiral'
  122
Phormium 47, 92
  P. tenax 80, 142
Pittosporum tenuifolium 76
plans 101–7, *102–6*
plants 73–92, 98
pleached trees 116, *117*, 118, *119*
poetry 14, *14*, *15*
Polygonatum biflorum 118
  P. × *hybridum* 76, *77*, 138
Polystichum setiferum 138
ponds 59, 60, 64, 66–8, 70, 116,
  132, 136

potagers 84–5
pots 42–4, *42–3*, 45
Pratia pedunculata 78
Primula 60
  P. florindae 60, 68, 138
privet 56
Prunus 'Shirotae' 134
  P. spinosa 122
Pulsatilla vernalis 146
pumps, water features 60–4

Q
Quercus ilex 142

R
raised beds 34, 116, *119*, 144, *145*
Ranunculus acris 138
retreats 38–40, *39–40*
rhododendrons 94
rills 59, *63*, 64, *65*, 70, *88*, 116,
  117, 128, *129*, 130
roof gardens 44, 124–6, *125*, *127*
Rosa (roses) *23*, 41, 89, 132
  R. 'Constance Spry' 134
  R. 'Eglantyne' 134
  R. 'Fragrant Memories' 134
  R. 'Gertrude Jekyll' 134
  R. 'Heritage' 134
  R. 'Korhassi' 78
  R. 'Madame Alfred Carrière' 122
  R. rugosa 138
Rosmarinus officinalis 76, 142
Rule of Ratio 12–14, *19*
Rumex acetosa 138
Ruta graveolens 130

S
safety, water features 69–70
Salvia officinalis Purpurascens Group
  76, 126
  S. × *sylvestris* 'Mainacht' 122
Sambucus nigra 122
sandy soils 94–5, 96
Santolina chamaecyparissus 86, 88

scent 132
Schoenoplectus lacustris subsp.
  tabernaemontani 'Zebrinus' 68
Scilla sibirica 122
sculptures 40, 42
seating 22, *32–3*, 33–6, 155
Sempervivum montanum 142
shady gardens 111
short, wide gardens 112
shrubs 98
Sissinghurst, Kent 74
Sisyrinchium striatum 142
sloping sites 22, 104, *105*, 113, 155
snowdrops *see Galanthus*
soil 92–7
Solanum crispum 122
Soleirolia soleirolii 76, 92, 118
Solidago 'Laurin' 146
Sorbus aria 'Lutescens' 134
  S. cashmiriana 134
south-facing gardens 111
spirals 107, 148
squares 107, 151, *151*
stepping stones 25
steps 155
streams 59, 70
suburban gardens 120–2, *120–3*
summer houses *39*, 40, *40*, 136,
  138, *138–9*
sunny areas 103, 111
surveying 101–4, *102–5*
sweet peas 41, 90, 134
swings 34–6
Syringa 'Président Grévy' 122

T
Taxus baccata (yew) *55*, 56, 76, 90,
  132, 134, *135*
tender plants 82, 92
terracing 113
terracotta containers 42
themed gardens 88–92
Tilia oliveri 118
timber, 155

benches 34, *35*
containers 44
decks 21–2, *21, 23*
obelisks 41
paths *31*
pergolas 36, *37*, 38
topiary 90, 132
trees *91*, 103, 113
  on boundaries 47
  formal style 146, *147*
  fruit trees 28
  pleached trees 116, *117*, 118,
    119
  shelter 50
  tree houses 40
  woodland gardens 134
triangular plots 108, *108*, 148–9,
  148–9
Trollius europaeus 68, 138, 146
Tropaeolum majus 130
Tulipa 'Greuze' 134
  T. 'Queen of the Night' 122
  T. 'Spring Green' 74
turf, laying 26

U
urns 42–3, *42*, 44, 47

V
vegetables 85, 128–30, *129*,
  131
Verbascum 'Gainsborough' 78
  V. olympicum 146
Veronica longifolia 122
  V.l. 'Alba' 118
Versailles tubs 44
views 48–50
  focal points 42, 43, *43*
  gates *54*
  long, narrow gardens 111–12, 152
  marking out gardens 110
  'windows' 57
Viola tricolor 78
Vitis vinifera *73, 76*

W
walls 34, 50–1, 52, *52*
water *58–71*, 59–70, 113
water lilies 60, *67*, 68
water plants 68
watering 42, 111, 130
Weigela florida 122
wheelchair-access gardens *143*,
  144–6
wide gardens 112
wild flowers 28
wildlife gardens 54, 136–8, *137–9*
willow *13*, 41, 48, 56–7
wind 43–4, 50, 103, 110
Wisteria 132
  W. sinensis 122, 134
woodland gardens 90, *91*, 132, *133*,
  134, *135*
Wright, Frank Lloyd 18

Y
yew *see Taxus baccata*

Z
Zantedeschia aethiopica
  'Crowborough' 68, *71*

Picture credits

The publishers would like to
thank the following for providing
photographs and for permission to
reproduce copyright material.
While every effort has been made
to trace and acknowledge all
copyright holders, we would like
to apologize should there have
been any errors or omissions.

Art Archive 92;
Bridgeman Art Library 18;
Nicola Browne 93t;
Jonathan Buckley 29t;
Country Life 27;
Edifice 51, 63b; EWA 21, 23, 49r;
Garden Matters 47, 83t, 83b;
Garden Picture Library 22 (Howard
Rice), 28 (Brian Carter), 37r, 46, 63r
(Lamontagne), 70, 75 (John Beedle),
80l & 80c (Howard Rice), 85;
David Gardner 17;
John Glover 10, 25, 30, 67, 72, 87,
93r, 114;
Harpur Garden Library 19, 35, 37b,
55, 56, 58, 63t, 69, 73, 93b, 99;
Andrew Lawson 1, 2t, 14 (Ian
Hamilton Finlay, Little Sparta), 15,
29b, 31, 33, 41, 52, 54, 61, 71, 76l
& c, 88, 89, 100, 115;
Le Scanff Mayer 59;
S & O Mathews 4;
Modern Garden Company 34;
Clive Nichols 2b, 20, 37t, 39, 43,
49t, 53, 57, 64, 65, 76r, 77, 79b & r,
81, 83t, 90, 91, 96, 97, 101, 154;
Hugh Palmer 45, 60;
Photos Horticultural 49b, 79t,
80r, 94;
Ali Ward 6;
Jo Whitworth 11, 32, 98;
Clare Wilks 13t, b & r.